Teacher — Education

THOSE WHO CAN

UNDERGRADUATE PROGRAMS TO PREPARE ARTS AND SCIENCES MAJORS FOR TEACHING

JOSEPH S. JOHNSTON, JR.
Vice President for Programs
Association of American Colleges

JANE R. SPALDING
Associate Director of Programs
Association of American Colleges

ROGER PADEN
Assistant Professor of Philosophy
George Mason University

ABBIE ZIFFREN
Visiting Associate Professor of Religion
George Washington University

ASSOCIATION OF AMERICAN COLLEGES, 1989

THIS WORK WAS SUPPORTED BY
THE ROCKEFELLER FOUNDATION

Photo sources:
Cover: David H. Kilper, Washington University
Opposite page 7: Joe Di Dio, National Education Association
Opposite page 23: Washington University
Opposite page 33: Herb Weitman, Washington University
Opposite page 53: Herb Weitman, Washington University
Opposite page 97: Joe Di Dio, National Education Association

Published by
Association of American Colleges
1818 R Street, NW
Washington, D.C. 20009

ISBN 0-911696-47-4

CONTENTS

THE AUTHORS

JOSEPH S. JOHNSTON, JR., is vice president for programs at the Association of American Colleges, where he oversees, among other initiatives, the development of AAC's new Curriculum Data Base on higher education and a series of national projects connecting liberal and professional education. He has a Ph.D. in English language and literature from the University of Chicago and an MBA from the Wharton School of the University of Pennsylvania. Author and coauthor of a number of books and articles, he has taught at Bryn Mawr College, Temple and Villanova universities and the University of Maryland–College Park. Formerly assistant to the president at Bryn Mawr College, a visiting examiner for the Educational Testing Service, and a research associate with the University of Pennsylvania's Higher Education Finance Research Institute, he has consulted with colleges, universities, and state and federal agencies. He serves on the board of visitors of the University of North Carolina–Asheville and the board of directors of the National Humanities Alliance.

JANE R. SPALDING is associate director of programs at AAC. A graduate of Boston University, she was formerly a high school German teacher in the Winchester, Massachusetts, public schools and an elementary school French teacher in Takoma Park, Maryland. She directs, among other AAC programs, the Consultation Assistance Service, the Two-year/Four-year Transfer Project, and a project aimed at internationalizing the curriculum through business-school/liberal arts collaboration. She also is involved with planning a partnership among Washington, D.C.-area colleges, universities, and schools, and she recently served as a consultant to the U.S. Department of Education on teacher education.

ROGER PADEN is an assistant professor of philosophy at George Mason University. A former assistant director of programs at AAC, he received his Ph.D. in philosophy from the University of Illinois at Urbana-Champaign. He has taught at the universities of Connecticut, Florida, and Maryland–College Park. The author of more than thirty scholarly articles and reviews, he has a special interest in applied philosophy.

ABBIE ZIFFREN is a visiting associate professor of religion at George Washington University. Editor, author, and translator of a number of publications, she has taught at Rutgers–The State University of New Jersey and the University of Wisconsin–Madison, from which she received her Ph.D. in South Asian Studies with a focus on religion and literature. Both as a research associate of the Urban Studies Center at Rutgers and as a reporter for several

New York and New Jersey area newspapers, she developed an expertise in the problems of inner-city schools. She also has served as a consultant to the chancellor of Rutgers on open-admissions programs for disadvantaged youths and to the school board of New Brunswick, New Jersey, on social studies curricula and in-service teacher training.

ACKNOWLEDGMENTS

Generous grant support from the Rockefeller Foundation has made possible the writing and publication of *Those Who Can*. Alberta Arthurs, the foundation's director for arts and humanities, first saw the need for such a project and suggested that the Association of American Colleges (AAC) undertake it. The authors warmly thank her and her colleagues—notably Steven D. Lavine, Susanna Miller, and Ellen S. Buchwalter—for the encouragement and assistance they have provided.

AAC is indebted as well to a strong project advisory committee. The positions taken in the text are not necessarily those of all committee members. The authors have benefited greatly, however, from the group's discussions and counsel and deeply appreciate their interest and support for the book's broad goals. Advisory committee members are:
□ Tomas A. Arciniega, President, California State College–Bakersfield
□ Denise Benskin, Faculty Member, Department of Foreign Languages, Duke Ellington School of the Arts, Washington, D.C.
□ Ronald Calgaard, President, Trinity University
□ Constance Clayton, Superintendent, Philadelphia Public Schools
□ George Drake, President, Grinnell College
□ Marilyn J. Guy, Chair, Education Department, Concordia College–Moorhead
□ Barbara Hatton, Dean, School of Education, Tuskegee Institute
□ Willis D. Hawley, Dean, George Peabody College for Teachers, Vanderbilt University
□ David Imig, Executive Director, American Association of Colleges for Teacher Education (AACTE)
□ Richard C. Kunkel, Executive Director, National Council for Accreditation of Teacher Education
□ Howard D. Mehlinger, Dean, School of Education, Indiana University–Bloomington
□ Joseph Phillips, Chair, English Department, Central High School, Philadelphia
□ Harold Raynolds, Jr., Commissioner of Education, Commonwealth of Massachusetts
□ Linda B. Salamon, Dean of the College of Arts and Sciences, Washington University
□ Albert Shanker, President, American Federation of Teachers, AFL-CIO
□ Robert E. Shoenberg, Special Assistant to the Vice President for Academic Affairs, University of Maryland–College Park
□ Marilyn Turkovich, Director, Urban Education Program, Associated Colleges of the Midwest

Four consultants contributed to the design and analysis of the 1987 survey of certification programs—the results of which (reported in Chapter Nine) have helped shape ideas presented throughout the book. Thomas Mangione, senior research fellow, Center for Survey Research, University of Massachusetts–Boston, reviewed a draft of the survey questionnaire and made helpful suggestions. Susan Shaman, associate director of the Institute for Research on Higher Education at the University of Pennsylvania, performed a formal statistical analysis of the returns. Our two primary advisors on the survey, however, were Michael Useem, professor of sociology and director of the Center for Applied Social Sciences at Boston University, and Ann Converse Shelly, professor of education and director of teacher preparation programs at Bethany College. Both were involved in every phase of survey planning and interpretation. Professor Shelly assisted us in our research on the professional component of teacher education as well. Her ideas on the subject inform many of the recommendations in Chapter Seven. We are indebted for other ideas and materials to Alan R. Tom, professor of education at Washington University, and to Penelope Engel, program associate with the Educational Testing Service.

Early drafts of the manuscript were read by Russell Edgerton, president of the American Association of Higher Education, as well as David Imig, Robert Shoenberg, and Ann Converse Shelly. We very much appreciate their time and interest. The book is better for their suggestions.

The efforts of many AAC staff members have been essential. John Chandler and Stanley Paulson had leading roles in developing the project—and the former in seeing it through. Carol Schneider and Harry Smith generously assisted at many points. With great skill Matthew Anderson processed survey returns. Sherry Levy-Reiner, Karen Poremski, and David Stearman ably oversaw the production of the volume itself, and Alexandra Maduros assisted in proofreading. Nora Topalian worked tirelessly entering a manuscript that evolved through many drafts.

Finally, *Those Who Can* is the product of an extensive and rewarding collaboration among its four authors. Roger Paden took a special responsibility for Chapter Eight, Jane Spalding for Chapter Nine, and Abbie Ziffren for Chapter Ten. The former two also helped edit and rework the manuscript as a whole. Jane Spalding also deserves special mention for helping direct the entire project and providing much of its research and administrative support.

It is a pleasure to acknowledge all these contributions. They have made possible what we hope will be a useful new resource for those concerned with improving the quality of our nation's teachers.
—JOSEPH S. JOHNSTON, JR.

CHAPTER ONE

■

INTRODUCTION

In the six years since the publication of *A Nation at Risk*, we have seen unprecedented efforts to strengthen the nation's public schools.[1] Some gains have been made. The overall quality of the schools, however, remains unacceptably low. Indeed, those who monitor such things debate whether the situation is one of stagnation or continuing decline.

More than any previous national school reform movement, that of the 1980s has "defined the quality of teachers as both the problem and the solution."[2] It is widely recognized that the best way to break the cycle by which ineffective teaching reproduces itself over generations is to improve dramatically the quality of teachers entering the system.[3] As a group, however, America's colleges and universities so far have failed to meet this challenge. Most recognize in principle some responsibility for the education of teachers, and many maintain a role. But aggressive, well-supported efforts are rare. Few institutions are trying seriously to recruit large numbers of more able students

into teaching or provide them with more challenging and substantive programs.

There are many reasons for higher education's under-performance. Institutional and academic leaders, of course, have other important priorities. Many simply are not well informed about the seriousness of the problem, and some, inevitably, regard it with indifference. But even those who are thoughtful and informed often have reservations about the appropriateness and feasibility of their institutions' becoming more involved. Many are unclear—perhaps uneasy—about the purposes and processes of teacher education and its fit with their institutions' goals. Many do not know their options—the kinds of specific strategies and programs that their institutions might consider in any effort to do more.

If college and university leaders are unsure whether and how best to address the problem, it may have to do with the nature of the national debate around these questions. We have had strong defenses of the teacher education major (though generally not as it now stands) and strong calls for its elimination. Some have argued that the pedagogical component is what needs fixing, others that the essential problem is that teachers get too little of the liberal arts. The two reports that have succeeded in capturing national attention—those of the Holmes Group and the Carnegie Forum—propose solutions of little help to those non-research institutions in which the vast majority of teachers have been and probably always will be prepared.[4] These proposals for extended programs also have crowded out consideration of other options of which all institutions need to be aware.

Against this background of continuing need and uncertainty, this monograph attempts to sort through and clarify the issues that have surrounded and impeded reform. The essential facts are clearer than they might seem. The shortage of able, well-prepared teachers is extremely serious. Colleges and universities have the power to address the problem effectively. There are compelling reasons why most should try to do so. There are also proven ways in which they can approach the task. Institutions interested in rethinking their commitment to the education of teachers and the programs

through which they pursue that goal will, we hope, find *Those Who Can* a useful resource. The book synthesizes much existing literature. It makes an argument as well: its case for recruiting and preparing a new population of students through more integrated programs suggests one important direction for higher education's efforts.

This book was written with colleges and universities of all types in mind—large and small, public and private, highly selective and less so. The kind of program it recommends can be implemented in virtually any institution that grants a baccalaureate degree in the arts and sciences and offers some kind of certification program; it can exist alongside conventional education majors and in institutions providing graduate programs in that field. The individuals we hope to reach include institutional and academic policy makers—chancellors, presidents, vice presidents, deans, curriculum committee chairs, and the like—especially academic leaders in the arts and sciences and in education. Other intended audiences include those who shape education policy on the federal and state levels and, on the campuses, liberal arts and education faculty members.

Those Who Can is organized in two parts. The first part, consisting of chapters one through six, presents several essential contexts for the recommendations put forward in more detail in part two, chapters seven through ten. Most readers will find it helpful to read parts one and two in order, but the format accommodates those who want to turn first to suggestions of specific strategies and programs.

The book begins its argument by documenting, in Chapter Two, the nation's continuing inability to secure from among its teacher education graduates enough teachers of the quality it needs. Chapter Three proposes that a primary national and institutional strategy—in addition to improving the status of teaching—therefore should be to tap into the much larger and able pool of students who major in the arts and sciences. These students should be involved as undergraduates in challenging programs that integrate study of the liberal arts and education. Purposeful efforts to interest these students in teaching may represent the best hope for increasing the number, quality, and diversity of tomorrow's teachers.

A consideration in Chapter Four of what teachers need to know and be able to do shows that they need an unusually broad education, in its entirety both liberal and professional. Simple calls for more liberal arts or more practice teaching abound. But this review confirms that we need a design for reform more com-

prehensive than these conventional and limited formulations. Chapter Five examines proposals that would bring liberal arts majors into teaching by placing teacher preparation on the graduate level. It examines the context in which these proposals have arisen, some of the assumptions they embody, and some of the consequences to which they might lead. Chapter Six acknowledges the very real obstacles that impede the implementation of the integrated undergraduate programs for which we argue. Relating these obstacles to attitudes and values deeply entrenched in the academy, it suggests that in their deep common interest, and in the fundamental complementarity of their aims, liberal arts faculty members and teacher educators can find a new rationale for cooperation.

The second part of this book, consisting of chapters seven through ten, turns to specific steps colleges and universities might consider in their efforts to build strong, integrated undergraduate programs to prepare liberal arts majors for teaching. Because institutions are diverse and have different strengths on which to build, we do not recommend any one program model. We describe instead a variety of strategies and tactics consistent with this overall approach.

As the second part of *Those Who Can* illustrates, an "integrated program" for arts and sciences majors who are prospective teachers can take many shapes. We mean by that term, however, a program that ideally has several broad characteristics. Each of its principal parts—general education, arts and sciences major, and professional education—is internally coherent. They also are carefully coordinated and, to an extent, merged with one another. The program emphasizes rigorous and sustained study in the arts and sciences. It also engages undergraduates with this subject matter in ways that specifically support their efforts to prepare themselves as teachers. Study in the liberal arts is improved for all students by a new attention to teaching and learning and to the processes—not merely the products—of disciplinary enquiry. It is improved for prospective teachers specifically by new opportunities for them to coordinate their work on subject matter with their reflection on pedagogy—to ground their consideration of how to teach in the demands and potentials of particular material. At the same time, professional courses are enriched. Perhaps fewer in number, but more powerful as vehicles for both theory and practice, they draw extensively on the subject matter and enquiry approaches of the liberal arts.

An integrated program, in short, does not leave to students the task of relating the disciplines they have studied to general prescriptions about teaching—of bringing together what their professors have not. Through means described in the second part of this book, an integrated program breaks down distinctions between liberal and professional study that subvert the best efforts to prepare teachers well.

The principal chapter of recommendations, Chapter Seven, ranges far beyond the professional education component to address general education and study in the major as well. It discusses supportive structures and administrative strategies and the transformation of the entire institution into a setting in which teaching and learning are taken seriously. The chapter concludes with brief sections on induction and in-service programs and on the importance of the states' allowing colleges and universities the freedom to fashion first-rate programs.

Chapter Eight gives sustained attention to the serious shortage of minority teachers. It indicates the many points in the "pipeline" at which we need to intervene and suggests a number of strategies. It is here that we discuss school/college partnerships and recruitment efforts in the schools and community colleges; these have important roles to play, however, in efforts to recruit and prepare students of all racial and ethnic backgrounds. Chapter Nine summarizes the results of a recent AAC survey of current practice in certification programs for arts and sciences majors. Since these programs can provide a foundation for the kind of programs envisioned in the text, this information is a benchmark against which to measure future progress. This chapter also identifies some of the arrangements and approaches most often associated with the more viable of the programs surveyed.

Chapter Ten presents brief descriptions of eleven programs that already have undertaken innovations of the sort we advocate. These initiatives at a diverse sample of colleges and universities demonstrate how much can be accomplished and how many shapes positive change can take. Finally, as an appendix, we include a list of selected organizations—in some cases, projects—from which readers can get current information about efforts now underway around the country to strengthen the education of teachers.

Our title alludes to that hoary, much-adapted, and originally Shavian axiom: "Those who can, do; those who cannot, teach." Well-educated liberal arts graduates are among "those who can." It is a high priority that we interest more of them in becoming teachers—some of society's most important "doers"—and prepare them well for their future roles.[5]

To hold this position, finally, is not to imply that teacher education programs fail to produce many able and well-prepared graduates. We are critical in these pages of professional education, but perhaps no more so than we are of the arts and sciences. Our general feeling is that undergraduate teacher education programs should be supported and strengthened. So long as a major in education incorporates essential characteristics of the integrated program we are recommending for arts and sciences majors, it has a role to play. The need for good teachers is too great to neglect any promising source. In the area of principal concern to us—the preparation of liberal arts majors for the schools—we see an extensive and essential role for teacher educators. Only when liberal arts and education faculties work together will colleges and universities develop the teacher preparation programs we need.

CHAPTER TWO

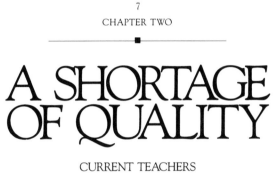

A SHORTAGE OF QUALITY

CURRENT TEACHERS

PROSPECTIVE TEACHERS

Our system of public schooling operates without any national locus of power or oversight. For the most part, support flows from and responsibility is vested in the fifty states, their educational agencies, and their more than fifteen thousand school districts. Any one of these may or may not collect (or report) certain kinds of information on schools, students, teachers, hiring, curricula, test scores, and the like. The information collected or reported may or may not lend itself to aggregation. As a result, we lack good data on many key elements of public education in this country and cannot answer with confidence a range of basic questions about it.

The same kind of problem frustrates efforts to examine the education and characteristics of prospective teachers in colleges and universities.

Undergraduates complete education majors or seek certification in more than twelve hundred U.S. institutions. The available information on these students and their programs is partial and of variable quality. Some future teachers elude educational researchers almost entirely by completing their degrees in fields other than education. Comprehensive data even on teacher education majors are surprisingly hard to come by.

Numerous national agencies, public and private, collect education statistics.[6] They have made considerable progress in recent years toward eliminating chronic deficiencies in our information base. But again, most have a partial view of data needs, and discrepancies turn up on every hand. The best advice may be that offered by one prominent researcher: "When it comes to education statistics, don't believe anything. No one knows."

It is not only inadequate information that makes it difficult to see American elementary and secondary education whole and describe it accurately. Ours is a truly universal system of public education, employing more than two million teachers in eighty-three thousand schools. The very diversity of the system would frustrate attempts at generalization even if our data were better. Whether one's concern is schools, teachers, or teacher education, the scale and variety of things ensures multitudes of exceptions.

We stress these caveats at the outset of a chapter that makes both extensive use of data and a number of critical generalizations. As a society concerned with its schools, we haven't the luxury to "not believe anything." We must work as best we can with the information we have, remembering its imperfections. Used cautiously, the available statistics do shed light on a variety of key issues. Some may find the conclusions they support depressing or think they are better left unsaid. And it is true that education-bashing, a popular blood-sport in the academy, serves no purpose. At the same time, it is important that the nation face the problems of its schools squarely. By looking at the nature and extent of some of those problems, we compre-

hend their seriousness and put ourselves in a better position to address them.

The series of national reports in the mid-1980s that sought to galvanize political support for school reform brought one issue in particular into prominence. The reports justified the need for change largely in terms of an impending shortage of teachers. Whatever the wisdom of tying the long-term agenda for change so closely to a rhetoric of crisis, this question of whether we will have enough teachers is important if only as a starting point for our discussion.

Many questions have been raised about the validity of the methods used to document claims of a teacher shortage. What Ernest Boyer aptly calls "the shoot-out over numbers" regarding teacher supply and demand has involved a number of combatants.[7] Some claim that traditional methods of projection give undue weight to graduates of education programs, ignoring arts and sciences and other graduates who complete certification as undergraduates, graduates of alternative certification programs, holders of emergency and provisional certificates, and the large number of former teachers who might be lured back to the classroom.[8] Some argue that the very attention directed to the purported shortage and the increases in teacher salaries that have ensued have already gone far toward correcting the problem. They point to substantial increases in the late 1980s in the number of first-year students declaring teaching as their intended career and, more recently, the numbers of undergraduates enrolling in education programs.

Using their different assumptions and methods, forecasters continue to reach disparate and difficult-to-reconcile conclusions. Emily Feistritzer of the privately supported National Center for Education Information reports that for the foreseeable future there will be more than enough applicants to fill available positions.[9] The Department of Education's National Center for Education Statistics provides little information about supply but predicts a pronounced rise in annual demand for new public school hiring, from 128,000 in 1988 to 174,000 in 1995.[10] Linda Darling-Hammond, a Rand Corporation researcher, projects a need for no fewer than 200,000 new teachers a year over the next six to seven years—a number almost twice that, she points out, of the new education graduates we now produce annually.[11]

Insofar as the key factor in projecting supply is interest in teaching on the part of *all* college students, Alexander Astin's surveys of first-year students are not encouraging,

either. The 8.8 percent of 1988 first-year students who plan to pursue careers in elementary or secondary schools compares well with the low of 4.7 percent who did so in 1982; yet, as Astin points out, the current level "still falls short of projected demand."[12] On balance, however, wide gaps in the available data, particularly on supply, would seem to make trustworthy projection of an overall shortage all but impossible.

We can predict with confidence, however, what Columbia University's Michael Timpane has called "distributional" shortages—shortages of certain kinds of teachers in certain subjects in certain kinds of schools and regions.[13] Although studies do not always agree on what these will be, they most frequently mention a net need for science (especially physics and chemistry), math, and computer science teachers and teachers equipped to provide bilingual and special education. They point to particular shortfalls of supply in the northeast and south central regions of the U.S. and to shortages of teachers willing and prepared to assume positions in the inner cities. Less often mentioned, but seen by many as a critical problem for the status of teaching as a profession, is a drastic shortage of males. Women represent more than two-thirds of current teachers and well in excess of three-quarters of stu-

Our concern is to review the evidence
that there is, and will continue to be,
a need for more highly qualified teachers

dents now preparing to teach. At the elementary level, female teachers outnumber their male counterparts five to one.[14] Finally, we can be sure of a worsening shortage of minority teachers—a problem so critical (and so resistant to easy solution) that we treat it at length in a separate chapter (see Chapter Eight).

The principal concern we want to explore in this chapter, however, is not the overall supply of teachers. Nor, as important as these matters are, do we focus on the need for teachers of particular subjects, for particular regions and schools, or of particular races and genders. Our concern is to review the available evidence that there is, and will continue to be, a need for more *highly qualified* teachers. Chapter Four considers what a "highly qualified" teacher might be; the notion is understood in many different ways. For now, we use a simple working definition: a bright, broadly educated individual who has command both of the subjects to be taught and of the ways in which they can be taught effectively to the range of students he or she will be teaching.

CURRENT TEACHERS

It is difficult to document with good national data a shortage of highly qualified teachers—as difficult as it is to confirm the other shortages we

have mentioned. Different kinds of evidence do suggest, however, that the nation's schools lack teachers of the caliber they need.

We begin with the National Assessments of Educational Progress (NAEP), a series of federally funded studies constituting "the nation's report card" on student knowledge in broad areas such as mathematics, science, literature, and United States history. These tests of student achievement are an indirect but important measure of teacher effectiveness, and they have much to tell us about what is and is not being accomplished in the schools.

The most recent (October 1987) NAEP report on literature and U.S. history focused on factual knowledge of high school juniors. It begins with the curiously optimistic observation that "the majority of students have at least some knowledge upon which they can build."[15] The report received much attention from the press, notably for its finding that nearly seven of ten high school juniors did not know the half-century when the Civil War occurred. The results as a whole, however, were mixed. About two-thirds of the survey questions about U.S. history were answered correctly by more than half the students. Levels of performance of the literature assessment were slightly lower.[16]

With U.S. colleges reporting in recent years a 10 to 30 percent rise in demand for remedial coursework in mathematics, few in higher education will be surprised by the results of NAEP's mathematics assessments. Although there have been improvements in average proficiency levels since 1978, these have been confined primarily to basic skills. "Discrepancies between the level of mathematics commonly taught in elementary, middle, and high schools and what students know...appear to increase over the school years," according to the report.[17] "Only about three-fourths of the nine-year-olds (third and fourth graders) showed beginning skills in understanding, only about two-thirds of the thirteen-year-olds (seventh and eighth graders) demonstrated skills universally taught in elementary school, and only about half the seventeen-year-olds performed at a level suggesting any sophisticated understanding of mathematics."[18]

The seriousness of the problem becomes apparent when one sees the questions posed. Mastery of "moderately complex procedures and reasoning" is tested by items such as, "Which of the following is true about 87 percent of ten?" The possible answers in this case—other than "can't tell" or "I don't know"—are that it is "greater than ten," "less than ten," and "equal to ten." The proportion of seventeen-year-olds ca-

pable of handling questions this difficult was 51.1 percent. Still more worrisome is the proportion showing a command of "multi-step problem-solving and algebra" demanded by questions such as the following: "Christine Barr borrowed $850 for one year from the Friendly Finance Company. If she paid 12 percent simple interest on the loan, what was the total amount she repaid?" Only 6.4 percent of seventeen-year-olds proved capable of answering such items correctly.[19] The report characterized the overall mathematical performance of many students as "dismal."[20]

"Distressing and alarming" and "a national disgrace" are phrases that have been used to describe the understanding of science revealed by elementary and high school students in the most recent *Science Report Card.*[21] Trends for nine-, thirteen-, and seventeen-year-olds across five assessments from 1969 to 1986 reveal a pattern of protracted decline followed by subsequent recovery for all age groups. The recoveries, however, have occurred only in the area of lower-level skills and basic science knowledge. They have not in any case matched the declines, especially for seventeen-year-olds. Most students in that age group were found to be "inadequately prepared either to perform competently jobs that require technical skills or to benefit substantially from specialized on-the-job training." Only 7 percent were prepared to handle college-level science courses.[22]

The comparative perspective provided by the 1988 report of the International Association for the Evaluation of Educational Achievement answers any suspicion that the NAEP and similar surveys hold U.S. students to unrealistic standards. This ranking of science achievement among elementary and secondary students in seventeen countries put American ten-year-olds eighth and fourteen-year-olds fourteenth. Among the thirteen countries that also tested high school students, U.S. twelfth graders ranked ninth in physics, eleventh in chemistry, and thirteenth in biology.[23] As the Duke of Burgundy has it in *Henry V* (V, ii, 56–58), "Our...children / Have lost.../ The sciences that should become our country."

Similar findings and patterns emerge from assessments of other kinds of mastery that we expect the schools to impart. A recent study done for the National Geographic Society found that young people now have much less overall knowledge of geography than did students in 1947—with, for instance, one in five eighteen- to twenty-four-year-olds now unable to find the United States on a world map.[24] The pattern of modest growth in basic skills with little or no progress in higher order reasoning abilities was apparent in the results of a 1988 NAEP reading assessment.[25] A study sponsored by the Joint Council of Economic Education found "shockingly" high levels of economic illiteracy. For example, fewer than half of high school juniors and seniors recognized that a government budget deficit is produced when government spending exceeds revenues. Just 34 percent knew that profits are the difference between a firm's revenues and its costs.[26]

Any attempt simply to ascribe the poor showing of U.S. students on these tests to their teachers would be mistaken. A multitude of factors combine to produce the failure these appraisals bring to light. School environments inimical to learning, lack of support from parents, underinvestment in education by society at large (and, indeed, by school systems)—these and other factors frustrate and compromise the efforts of the best classroom teachers. It is even possible (if unlikely) that these results speak of great success on the part of teachers, given what we ask of them and what they have to work with. There is evidence, however, that takes us a step closer to isolating the effectiveness of teachers, and that is the growing literature reporting observation of their performance in the classroom.

Albert Einstein once wondered that our "methods of instruction have not entirely strangled the holy curiosity of inquiry."[27] That observation squares fairly well with what we know about the typical practice of classroom teachers. John Goodlad has found that 70 percent of all classroom time is spent with the teacher speaking and the children listening passively. In a day filled with "teacher talk," active forms of learning are only rarely encouraged.[28] Other research shows that in conventional classrooms teachers do fully 90 percent of the work. When surveyed, they constantly underestimate what they do and overestimate what they require of their students.[29]

Many of the deficiencies revealed by the NAEP surveys apparently can be traced to prevailing styles of instruction. Reading, for instance, is still too often taught using "readers," which, as William Honig has observed, "there is no reason to read."[30] This practice, moreover, is part of a more general dependence on textbooks and guides. Clearly it is not the fault of the teachers that today's textbooks, with their "pointlessly arid writing" and "dumbed-down content," more often than not "confuse, mislead and profoundly bore."[31] Yet many of these teachers are trained and required to rely on prescribed materials and procedures precisely because of a fundamental distrust of teachers that often is warranted by their variable quality. Indeed, as we shall see, some are probably glad enough to depend on these "teacher-proof" materials, because their college years have left them unprepared to do otherwise.[32]

Those who have looked closely at mathematics instruction report classrooms "more concerned with students' rote use of procedures than with their understanding of concepts and development of higher-order thinking skills."[33] Although typically seen as a forbidding structure of rules needing to be mastered, math is in fact a rich and powerful "symbolic language invented...and [evolving] as new needs arise."[34] It lends itself to inductive approaches and real-world applications, and its study can be enlivened by a range of instructional technologies, including calculators and computers. Yet math generally is taught in our schools, writes Edward Fiske, "as revealed truth...a view [that] of course dovetails nicely with 'teacher talk' as the basic classroom technique."[35] What active component there is to a student's experience of the subject too often is confined to textbook-based pencil-and-paper drills. Appropriate technologies are used too seldom and often are entirely unavailable.[36]

Science instruction, too, continues to be lecture- and textbook-dominated.[37] The achievement of scientific understanding is clearly related to experimentation—the "doing" of science in a way that emphasizes its inquiry processes as much as its conclusions. However, the percentage of teachers using hands-on activities dropped, depending on the grade, between 15 and 27 percent during a recent ten-year period. In 1986, for example, a National Science Foundation study found that the share of high school science courses including some form of laboratory exercise was an alarmingly low 39 percent.[38] A more urgent problem, however, may be the small exposure students get to science education of any kind. A recent study shows that elementary (K–3) school teachers spend an average of only eighteen minutes per day teaching science.[39] For most students the study of science stops completely in the tenth grade.[40] With only 15 percent of American high school students electing to study physics and only 30 percent electing to study chemistry, they receive as a group only one-half to one-third the exposure to science that their counterparts in other developed countries receive.[41]

The reasons for the situation are numerous and complex, but it is widely conceded that they include the inadequacies of teachers themselves. Unable to arouse and channel the natural curiosity of young children about the world around them,

too many teachers in the elementary schools "seem to succeed primarily in conveying their own anxiety and negative attitudes about [science]."[42] In the process, of course, they reduce the numbers of students interested in learning more.

Reports on teaching in other fields sound similar themes. The NAEP in literature and U.S. history found "a very traditional approach to instruction."[43] In the latter field, for example, teachers typically rely heavily on their textbooks. Only occasionally do they introduce supplementary readings or make any reference to original documents.[44] Geography, like history, is an important subject too often subsumed—to its peril— under "social studies." Also like history, it is a subject too few teachers know well or know how to teach. Its current presentation in the schools has been characterized as "trivial pursuits" and as "a bland, monotonous blend of names and places, intellectually stimulating to neither students nor teachers."[45]

We emphasize that we speak on average, drawing from studies and reports which have found large numbers of highly competent and effective teachers in every field and grade level. It also bears repeating that instructional effectiveness itself is a function of many variables. One cannot use laboratory equipment that does not exist. It is difficult, in a rule-directed setting, to depart from a prescribed curriculum—no matter how much student learning requires it. Nonetheless, the indirect evidence we have reviewed thus far does at least raise questions about the quality of the teaching force itself—about its general ability levels, subject matter preparation, and pedagogical skill. We continue, then, to several kinds of evidence that speak more directly still to the attributes of current teachers themselves.

One such type of evidence has to do with the educational backgrounds of teachers—what they have studied and at what levels. Although more than half of U.S. teachers now have master's degrees, the overwhelming majority of these degrees are in education.[46] Many of these degrees, moreover, have been granted in areas like administration and counseling, whose appeal to those getting them lies principally in their promise as foundations for better paying careers beyond the classroom. Since few teachers have been rewarded for pursuing advanced knowledge in the subjects they teach, few have done so. Most teachers draw their understanding of their fields from what they learned as undergraduates—five, ten, twenty, or thirty years ago.

Most teachers have their undergraduate degrees in education as well. Those who have entered the profession in the 1980s, moreover,

are even more likely than their predecessors to have completed their baccalaureates in that field. As recently as 1980, 34 percent of new college graduates who were certified to teach had completed baccalaureate degrees in the arts and sciences; by 1984 that number had fallen precipitously to 19 percent. The percentage of newly certified education graduates who actually enter teaching is substantially higher than the percentage of newly certified arts and sciences graduates who do so; thus, education majors may be even more dominant in the teaching force than these numbers suggest.[47]

Insofar as breadth of education and subject matter mastery are concerned, this traditional dominance of the education major has conferred great importance upon the coursework that teachers have completed within the liberal arts. Typically, the available information allows for few definitive statements about the scope and nature of this coursework. Nonetheless, what we do know about the general education and liberal arts preparation received by education graduates now in the schools suggests room for improvement. One study by the Southern Regional Education Board (SREB) examined the transcripts of six thousand education and arts and sciences majors who graduated in 1982–83 from a group of seventeen major institutions in fourteen southern states. The study found that, compared with their peers in the arts and sciences, graduates in education completed fewer general-education credits; less of what they did take, moreover, was truly college-level or upper-level coursework. Although they completed more credits in psychology, fine arts, biology, and geology, they took, on average, fewer hours in mathematics, English, physics, chemistry, economics, history, political science, sociology, other social sciences, foreign languages, philosophy, and other humanities.[48]

The problem highlighted by the SREB study seems to be in part that many institutions have lacked appropriately extensive general education requirements. Nonetheless, many graduates in education have not taken enough additional liberal arts coursework to compensate—or, in some cases, to acquire even the subject matter knowledge from cognate fields essential to their teaching. A 1985–86 study supported by the National Science Foundation found, for example, that fewer than half of secondary science teachers have ever taken a college course in computer science, and almost half have had no college calculus. At the elementary level, only one in three science teachers have had a college chemistry course, and only one in five a college course in physics.[49]

Academic ability is not everything in a teaching career—any more than is the coursework one has completed. It is, however, an important variable. Looking at the general academic aptitude of teachers, we find ourselves on familiar ground: with limited information, the best of it imperfect, but no reason to doubt the generally unfavorable conclusions to which it points. A recent large-scale study that breaks out scores of different populations on the 1986–87 Graduate Record Examination suggests a clear pattern. The study reports the mean verbal, quantitative, and analytical scores of all test takers intending to pursue graduate work in each of eleven areas. Those test takers planning to pursue a master's (but not doctoral) degree in education—the vast majority of whom we can assume to be teachers—achieved the lowest scores of any cohort intending graduate study. They ranked tenth of eleven in verbal (with a mean score of 447 as compared to the mean of 469 for all cohorts), eleventh in quantitative (with 457 as compared with 520), and eleventh in analytical (with 479 as compared with 514).[50]

An equally worrisome picture emerges from the same data when one looks at the performance of those who listed education as their undergraduate major relative to that of those who listed undergraduate majors in other fields. Education majors ranked last—eleventh of eleven—on all three sections (verbal, quantitative, and analytical) among all students intending graduate study, as well as among those intending graduate study specifically in education.[51] What we can learn from standardized test scores is, of course, limited. Yet it is a mistake to ignore them. They cannot indicate who should teach, but they may indicate who should not.[52]

These findings about the caliber of teachers now in the schools square well with conclusions reached in an extensive 1986 review of research on teacher education by Judith Lanier and Judith Little. Teaching, they write, "does attract and retain many very bright people [but also gets] too many persons with excessively low scores on academic measures." Over the decade 1976–86, the "preservice" pool became substantially smaller, but it also was "composed of fewer academically talented and more academically weak students" than previously—a change of no small concern given the substantial numbers of preservice students who "traditionally scored in the lowest quartile of measured college student ability."[53] To this sobering fact we need to add one more to appreciate the pool that now supplies the nation's classroom. During that same decade, according to Lanier and Lit-

tle, academically talented teachers left the profession in disproportionate numbers, and disproportionate numbers of the less academically talented were retained. The academic talent in recent years has thus tended to sort itself out of teaching, leaving group norms for practicing teachers to fall toward the low-to-average end of the scale.[54]

PROSPECTIVE TEACHERS

Some would reply to such data that it has always been so. A dearth of high quality teachers has, after all, been "a topic of expressed frustration and discussion...since the 1800s."[55] A more pertinent objection might be that reforms in the last few years have addressed key causes of the problem and that the necessary correction is, in the late 1980s, already underway.

Indeed, much change has come about in the wake of the school reform movement essentially begun with *A Nation at Risk* in 1983 and shaped more recently by the growing literature, including the Holmes and Carnegie reports, on the reform of teacher education. Most of this change has resulted from what is sometimes termed the "first wave" of reform—the legislative and regulatory mandates developed as states responded in the mid-1980s to the perceived crisis in the schools. Many

We need to take a clear-eyed look
at the characteristics of prospective teachers...
on whom we now are pinning our hopes
of strengthening the teaching force

states increased requirements for high school graduation, stiffened standards for entry into teacher education programs and for certification, introduced alternative routes of certification for those already holding college degrees, and/or increased teacher salaries (restoring the national average salary to real dollar levels last seen in the early 1970s).[56]

Advocates of school reform correctly have insisted on the need for a "second wave" of reform that would address more fundamental and intractable problems having to do with the status and professionalism of teachers. Meanwhile, however, the results of this "first wave" have been visible. According to one report, student interest in teaching increased 66 percent during the years 1982–87.[57] Colleges of education report increased enrollments and higher-quality students.[58] The proportion of new teachers saying they expect to leave the profession within five years has declined, and more parents now indicate that they would like their children to pursue careers in teaching.[59]

History tells us there is a pendular quality to the nation's attention to its schools. Perceptions of crisis prompt concern and then action; as we get results, concern soon wanes, giving rise to the neglect that in time breeds crisis anew. If current reform efforts are to lead to changes of

real consequence, we cannot simply assume that recent and current reforms are sufficient or that positive trends, left to run their course, will take care of our problems. We need to take a clear-eyed look at the characteristics of *prospective* teachers— those who have been drawn to the profession and are completing college in an environment of school reform—those on whom we now are pinning our hopes of strengthening the teaching force.

There have been a number of studies of prospective teachers in recent years. Several portray education majors in very positive terms. Most of these are local studies, however, and some reflect a clearly defensive posture. A review of the most broadly based studies suggests that, while there has been progress, teaching still is not attracting aspirants of the quality and diversity it needs. Teacher educators are among those most concerned with this fact and have, indeed, taken the lead in documenting the nature and extent of the problem.

A 1987 report by the American Association of Colleges for Teacher Education (AACTE) provides an overall profile of undergraduate secondary education methods students. It describes a population that is 89 percent white and 75 percent female. The education students are said to be of "average" verbal and mathematical ability as measured by SATs. Forty percent are transfer students. They are, like most college students, monolingual, and half attend college within fifty miles of home. Most (including the minority students) are from suburban and rural backgrounds, and overwhelming majorities prefer to return to such settings. Seventy-five percent wish to teach in a traditional classroom in a traditional school in a middle-income neighborhood with children of average ability. They show little interest in teaching students with handicaps or low ability or children from low-income backgrounds.[60]

Another 1987 AACTE report gives a relatively favorable account of the academic strength of prospective teachers. This study of those who entered colleges of education in 1984 and 1985 describes a population drawn from the top quarter of the high school class and with slightly above-average SAT scores (from 927 to nearly 1000, depending on their specialties within education). The average student is said to maintain a 2.9 grade point average through his or her first two years and to amass 135 credits before graduation.[61]

Other research, however, is less encouraging with respect to the intellectual profile of prospective teachers. These studies describe attitudes toward learning that are "instrumental and vocational" in nature.[62] On average, education majors do not see arts and sciences courses as relevant to their education as teachers and "show less interest in general education" than other students.[63] The suggestion is one of a general lack of interest in intellectual matters, whatever their curricular origin. These students are said to dismiss the theoretical components even of their education majors—which, as a whole, they regard as having little to teach them.[64]

The annual Cooperative Institutional Research Program (CIRP) surveys of "The American Freshman" performed by Alexander Astin and his associates at the University of California–Los Angeles are a particularly good source of information on the undergraduate population now pointing itself toward the teaching profession. The figures for fall 1988 first-year students indicate a rising student interest in teaching, with 8.8 percent planning teaching careers in the elementary and secondary schools. Although this represents an increase from a low of 4.7 percent in 1982, it represents only a .7 percent increase over last year and indicates a moderation of the widely reported six-year trend. Astin and his colleagues correctly emphasize that the level of interest falls far short of projected demand and is well below the all-time high of 23.5 percent.[65]

The recent rising interest in teaching also "masks some important trends regarding which students plan teaching careers and at what levels and in what fields." Virtually all entering students who aspire to careers in teaching now plan majors in education; conversely, there is "virtually no interest in careers in teaching... among freshmen planning liberal arts majors." This situation contrasts starkly with that of twenty-one years ago, when the majority of those planning to teach also planned majors in the arts and sciences.[66]

A related trend has been the decreasing interest in secondary school teaching. Only 3.2 percent of American first-year students now intend to teach in the nation's junior high and high schools, versus a high of 14.4 percent twenty-one years ago.[67]

A 1987 analysis of CIRP data conducted by Ronald Opp sheds more light on current college students who intend to teach. Looking at the self-ratings of first-year students interested in a variety of careers, Opp found that the percentage of aspiring teachers rating themselves "above average or in the top ten percent" on a wide variety of traits has decreased substantially since 1966 and lagged well behind the percentage of entering students in other fields doing so. On every trait examined—academic ability, drive to achieve, leadership ability, public speaking, intellectual self-confidence, mathematical ability,

social self-confidence, and writing ability—fewer of those intending to teach rated themselves highly than did students on other career tracks. On the other hand, more said that improving their reading or study skills was a very important reason for deciding to go to college. All these disparities, concludes Opp, "suggest that prospective teachers do not regard themselves [as being] as academically well prepared as freshmen in other careers."[68]

This profile is consistent with another finding of the 1988 CIRP report. First-year students intending to enter teaching are, in disproportionate numbers, pursuing their education in less selective colleges and universities. Within any given type of institution—all four-year Catholic colleges, or all public universities, for example—the percentage of first-year students wanting to teach in the schools drops as the institutional selectivity level increases from low to high. This basic result holds true whether one looks at male or female first-year students, and the steepest declines are seen when one looks at progressively more selective private institutions. Whereas, for example, 7.4 percent of first-year women in private universities classified as having "low selectivity levels" intend to teach, only 1.8 percent of first-year women in highly selective private universities intend to do so.[69]

It is, finally, by reference to high school seniors that we can make our most forward-reaching projections regarding the teaching force of the future. Students taking the SAT are asked to indicate their intended major. Comparison of mean SAT verbal and math scores of high school seniors intending to major in education with those of their peers intending other majors reveals an unfortunate but now-predictable pattern. In 1985, the former group's mean combined scores lagged the latter group's by an average of 72 points. Since then, this gap has closed somewhat, though by successively smaller increments. In 1988, a gap of 55 points remained.[70] SAT-takers also provide information on their rank in class. Although in 1988 the cohort intending majors in education surpassed fine arts and vocational majors, it has consistently reported a mean rank in high school class lower than that of most students with other academic plans.[71]

The available evidence does suggest, then, a shortage of high-quality teachers, both now and in the future. If the needs of our schools are to be met, colleges and universities will have to undertake the two broad interrelated types of effort on which this report focuses. They must provide prospective teachers baccalaureate educations that will ensure their effectiveness in the classroom. First, however, they must increase the number, quality, and diversity of those interested in becoming teachers. This challenge—recently termed by Ernest Boyer "the number one priority of [the] nation"—is the focus of the next chapter.[72]

CHAPTER THREE

EXPANDING THE POOL

IMPROVING THE STATUS AND PROFESSIONALISM
OF TEACHERS

TAPPING NEW SOURCES

WHY ARTS AND SCIENCES MAJORS?

The best efforts of colleges and universities to recruit more—and more able—people for careers in teaching will have little success unless teaching is in the meantime made a more attractive career. States and local school districts should continue, and in some cases step up, their efforts to improve salaries. They also must do more than most have considered doing to improve working conditions and enhance the professional status of teachers.

IMPROVING THE STATUS AND PROFESSIONALISM OF TEACHERS

Teaching has a relatively "flat" career path. Compensation structures in most states traditionally have provided for a salary differential of less than $10,000 between the highest- and lowest-paid classroom teachers.[73] Salary increases, moreover, have been concentrated in the first third of the career, providing little financial incentive for teachers to improve their performance during the remaining twenty-five to thirty years they teach.[74] It is often said that teaching is a career in which, if one wants to move *up*, one must move *out*—out of the classroom. School systems have long backlogs of teachers with masters' degrees in administration, counseling, and similar fields waiting for opportunities to make such moves and thereby begin earning higher wages.

The difficulty of attracting and retaining classroom teachers may have

The difficulty of attracting and retaining classroom teachers may have less to do with low salaries than with deplorable working conditions

less to do with low salaries, however, than with deplorable working conditions. Today's teachers spend an average of 40 percent of their work day on noninstructional tasks.[75] Often expected to teach 125 to 175 students a day, they have to put up with too many interruptions and complete too much paperwork–in addition, in many cases, to monitoring halls, planning pep rallies, collecting lunch money, sponsoring student clubs, and the like. They may have to grade papers and plan lessons on the evenings and weekends–a time when many work at second jobs to supplement their incomes. Most teachers have no office, no phone, no secretarial assistance, and no access to the office technologies the rest of us take for granted.[76] Working conditions leave them little time to give special attention to students who need it or to reflect on their teaching either alone or with other teachers. Certainly the norms of the staff room discourage substantive discussions; "everyone needs a break from the kids."[77]

As essential as it is to improve salaries and working conditions, reform efforts will get at the heart of the problem only when they give teachers more authority over what they do. Teachers are not fully vested professionals. Judgment and choice– even the freedom to improvise–are essential in the classroom.[78] Yet

teachers in many cases are increasingly rule-directed and use materials designed to limit their discretion. Although some teachers do help choose textbooks and shape curricula, their participation in decision making rarely extends much further. According to a recent report from the Carnegie Foundation, few teachers "participate in selecting teachers and administrators [or are] involved in such crucial matters as teacher evaluation, staff development, budget, student placement, promotion and retention policies, and standards of student conduct."[79] Until teachers are granted more autonomy and more voice in key decisions that affect their classrooms and their schools, teaching will not be a profession, as most people understand that term, and schools will continue to fare poorly in the competition for college talent.

Correcting these problems is urgent but difficult. Despite five years of the "school reform" movement, the overwhelming majority of teachers report that working conditions have not improved. Almost half say that their morale actually has declined over that period.[80] The problem has much to do with the difficulty of fashioning solutions that address the problems of low salaries, poor working conditions, and lack of professional autonomy in a fair and comprehensive way. Simple merit-pay schemes have proved difficult to administer equitably, and teachers tend to distrust them. At least twenty-four states, however, are experimenting with career ladders that tie some form of evaluation to opportunities for professional development, employment on different career tracks ("differentiated staffing"), and/or increased salary, "master teacher" designations, and other rewards.[81] Differentiated staffing has the particular advantage of providing scope to individual interests and abilities. It builds on one teacher's strength, for example, by enabling him to work as a mentor to beginning teachers, and on another's by encouraging her to be a scholarly resource in a discipline. Arrangements like these encourage autonomy in the most effective way possible: by developing teacher expertise.

All such reforms face obstacles, however. They may be expensive, raise measurement problems, entail significant reductions in bureaucracy, or require the revision of school codes. Predictably, in some places proposals to extend the authority of teachers are being opposed by groups—principals, curriculum specialists, school boards, and teacher associations—that see in them a threat that their own powers will be diminished.[82] Again, however, such reforms are essential conditions to the long-term ability of colleges and

universities to recruit better students to teaching and provide better teachers to the schools. To the extent that higher education can support these changes, it should.

Before turning to what higher education itself can do to increase the flow of more highly qualified teachers into the schools, we need to note the existence of so-called "alternative" and "irregular" certification programs designed to give interested individuals with college degrees, but without certification, an efficient route into teaching. These programs vary in nature and quality. Some are mounted by schools, colleges, and departments of education. Others, usually state- and district-sponsored, de-emphasize "professional coursework" in favor of on-the-job training. The teacher education community generally regards the latter with some suspicion. It argues that they are essentially apprenticeships, insufficient as preparation for the classroom, and that they represent an attempt to bypass responsible teacher education.[83] The teacher unions also have criticized these programs harshly.[84] On the other hand, the U.S. Department of Education has sponsored studies that have given nontraditional certification generally high marks for attracting candidates who are well prepared in their fields and giving them "more classroom experience and more intense supervi-

The pool must be enlarged from
a new source.... The population
of arts and sciences majors
is the source we most need to tap

sion" than traditional programs.[85] At
least some sources report that the
programs attract candidates who—
compared to traditional education
graduates—are more mature, more
sophisticated, better educated, and
more diverse in background.[86]

Although thirty-nine states either
have or are considering some form
of alternative or irregular certification, the long-term effectiveness of
these programs is still unclear.[87] They
may well have a helpful role to play.
But they are in any case unlikely
ever to supply more than a very
small fraction of the teachers needed
in the schools. The primary responsibility for recruiting and preparing
teachers will be with our colleges
and universities, where it now is
lodged—and largely neglected.

TAPPING NEW SOURCES

What, then, can institutions themselves do to enlarge the pool of prospective teachers? Since strong
students are always drawn to and retained by intellectually demanding,
high-quality curricula, we clearly
need to enrich and otherwise improve the college and university programs in which we educate teachers.
But—as we contend in the remainder
of this chapter—we must at the same
time reorient our recruiting efforts
themselves to new and promising
populations.

In Chapter Eight we describe a
number of successful efforts to recruit and build a better understanding of teaching in the schools and
community colleges. These kinds of
efforts should be given the most serious consideration (and adequate support) by every university or college
that educates teachers.[88] If only by
increasing the numbers of students
applying to conventional teacher education programs and allowing these
programs to be more selective, efforts
like these can increase the quality of
those in training.

Institutions seriously interested in
improving the numbers and quality
of those whom they prepare for
teaching, however, should see this
kind of recruitment as only one of
several possible solutions. They may
find another approach—preparing
arts and sciences majors for teaching—more effective and far-reaching.
What we mean by preparing arts
and sciences majors for teaching requires explanation, particularly for
those who think about the education of teachers in terms of current
practice.[89] Let us clarify in broad
terms how the idea represents a de-
parture both from the status quo
and from other proposals and why it
holds such promise for strengthening
the teaching force.

First, it is true that many students
preparing for careers in the secondary schools—where some think sub-

ject matter expertise more critical—traditionally complete majors in the arts and sciences. There are no reliable statistics on the percentage who do so, however, and, as we have seen, few current first-year students who intend to teach declare any intention of majoring in the arts and sciences voluntarily.[90] Although we would like to know how many of those now preparing for high school teaching do major in liberal arts disciplines, and although we would encourage more to do so, the issue is secondary to our concern here.

Our proposal looks to a different population—students who traditionally study in the arts and sciences with no thought of entering the elementary or secondary school classroom, or perhaps even with some aversion to the idea of doing so. It is essential to interest many more of these undergraduates in teaching. The current pool of prospective teachers is insufficient in size and quality regardless of the curricular channels through which it is supplied to the schools. The pool itself must be enlarged from a new source—one that can improve its quality. For a number of reasons, which we turn to shortly, the population of arts and sciences majors is the source we most need to tap.

We should distinguish this proposal from one that has come from other quarters. The Holmes Group

and the Carnegie Forum, among others, have proposed that teacher education be moved to the graduate level. This move would ensure undergraduate arts and sciences majors for all teachers; as with alternative certification programs, however, it would provide them with professional training only after graduation. Our proposal, by contrast, is that arts and sciences majors be recruited and prepared for teaching not after they have graduated but while they are pursuing their undergraduate studies. It is, as we shall explain, a call to involve them in four-year baccalaureate programs that integrate academic preparation in the liberal arts and professional training in education.

Not all elements of this approach would be new. Many colleges and universities already offer paths to certification for students majoring in arts and sciences. As we report in Chapter Nine, many do so at the undergraduate level. What has not been widely realized, however, is the power of a strategy that taps more aggressively into that pool of talent while providing challenging and integrated programs of study.

Most other approaches are easier. To achieve integrated programs for arts and sciences students, teacher educators and liberal arts faculty members must raise their sights, reexamine their attitudes and programs, and begin to work together in recognition of larger common concerns. Difficult as it is, however, this approach can do more than any other over the long term to increase the number of highly qualified teachers in the nation's schools. We turn now to a set of key reasons for thinking this to be the case, having to do with the size, quality, and other characteristics of the arts and sciences major population.

WHY ARTS AND SCIENCES MAJORS?

While the numbers of U.S. college and university graduates taking their degrees in education plummeted 51 percent between 1970-71 and 1985-86, the numbers graduating with majors in arts and sciences fell by a relatively modest 17.6 percent. Thus, although enrollments in the arts and sciences—including the natural sciences and mathematics, social sciences, humanities, and the arts—were affected by the well-publicized student preprofessionalism of recent years, they were affected less than were education enrollments by the decline of interest in teaching. The ratio of arts and sciences majors to education majors—about 2.4 to 1 in 1970—had actually grown by 1986 to nearly 4 to 1.[91]

These numbers alone suggest a primary reason for targeting arts and sciences students for careers in teaching. Even a relatively modest increase in the number of arts and science majors recruited would represent a very significant addition to the pool of teachers in training. Statistical breakdowns on students who major in the arts and sciences reveal something important, moreover, that the aggregate numbers obscure. This group includes its full share of those most critically needed in teaching and least well-represented in teacher education programs. The 1984-85 pool of degree recipients in the arts and sciences—again, nearly four times larger overall than that in education—included, for example, three and one-half times as many blacks, almost five times as many black men, and more than seven times as many men in all ethnic categories. Increasing the number of arts and sciences majors who prepare for teaching could dramatically increase the number of future teachers of now underrepresented races and gender.[92]

The pool of arts and sciences majors is promising, then, in its potential for increasing the overall numbers of prospective teachers as well as those from several underrepresented subgroups. It presents an important opportunity for increasing quality as well. Any major increase in the number of applicants will allow teacher preparation programs to be more selective. But there is in this case an additional reason why this would be so: the relatively high ability level of arts and sciences majors. Let us take a closer look at the standardized test and class rank results alluded to in the previous chapter.

The figure below presents mean combined SAT verbal and math data for the year 1988. Scores are presented by the intended major fields of the test-takers, all of them high school seniors. The scores for students interested in majoring in education can be compared here with the scores both of all examinees and of students intending to take their degrees in a variety of arts and sciences fields. Those specifically declaring themselves premedical and prelaw students are excluded.

The range of scores for students intending to major in arts and sciences is broad; most scores, however, are substantially above those of the intended education majors. We should, of course, be careful in ascribing relatively high ability levels to arts and sciences majors on the basis of scores and intentions of high

SAT VERBAL AND MATH SCORES OF HIGH SCHOOL SENIORS, 1988

INTENDED COLLEGE MAJOR	VERBAL	MATH	COMBINED
Education	407	442	849
Selected arts and sciences:			
Humanities	515	510	1025
History and culture	491	492	983
Psychology	440	463	903
Mathematics	468	596	1064
Chemistry	495	565	1060
Physics	539	621	1160
Biology	475	524	999
Economics	502	565	1067
Political science	501	517	1019
Foreign languages	479	499	978
Studio/performing arts	429	449	878
Sociology	411	432	843
All examinees	428	476	904

SOURCE: Jerilee Grandy, *Trends in SAT Scores and Other Characteristics of Examinees Planning to Major in Mathematics, Science, or Engineering* (Princeton, N.J.: Educational Testing Service, 1989), Tables 6, 10, 20, and 22.

school seniors. However, the GRE results reported in Chapter Two suggest that the broad orderings seen on the SAT tend not to change greatly as one looks farther down the pipeline at the cohorts emerging from college.[93]

These data suggest, then, a population of students majoring in the arts and sciences that is large, diverse, and, by standard academic measures, able relative to that in teacher education. To these traits we can add at least two more. First, to judge by studies reported in the previous chapter, arts and sciences majors may be on average more interested in "the content areas," the fields of academic study taught in the schools. One can easily assume too much about the intellectual curiosity of arts and sciences majors—forgetting, for example, how many have eyes only for what they need for a career. But for every such liberal arts student, there may be another who "gladly would learn" and, with encouragement, might "gladly teach" as well.

The second characteristic is that students majoring in the arts and sciences often are more open than others to different career directions. They tend disproportionately not to have committed yet to a life's work. Many students choose the arts and sciences because study in these fields leaves many options open and allows

broad-ranging exploration. Although some liberal arts students are genuinely ineffectual, "undecidedness"— as it is termed in student services circles—is in most cases a form of information gathering and mature deliberation. It should never be mistaken as academic weakness. Indeed, as Bernard Gifford, dean of the Graduate School of Education at the University of California-Berkeley, has noted, "Students who make an early decision to pursue studies in education at the undergraduate level (vertical recruits) are usually less academically able than students who make the decision to go into teaching later in their academic lives (lateral recruits)."[94]

As Gifford goes on to note, the number of these lateral recruits is now minuscule. Although students majoring in the liberal arts are numerous, diverse, able, engaged with their subjects, and uncommitted to other careers, they are not in substantial numbers deciding to become teachers. Why? Salary, status, and working conditions are certainly parts of the answer. The failure of many teacher education programs to mount effective recruiting efforts is another. Also at the heart of the problem, however, are issues of program structure and quality.

The sequence of education courses required for certification stands apart from, and must be completed in addition to, one's major and general education. It is sometimes difficult within four years to fit everything in. To take the sequence is also to ignore the prevailing wisdom about education courses—that, divorcing technique from content, they too often are trivial and irrelevant. It may be to ignore subtle discouragement or outright dissuasion from one's professors. It may be, some teacher educators themselves say, to study with students whose norms discourage the intellectually facile.[95] Little wonder that strong students sometimes ask, in the words of one from Brown University, why "the decision to teach in our society is analogous with the decision to stunt one's growth."[96]

Clearly there are strong programs in teacher education, including ones that attract arts and sciences majors and provide training of very high quality to them. Even according to many teacher educators, however, such programs are the exception. By and large, arts and sciences majors regard teacher education as a thing to be avoided or, if taken, to be endured. A sequence that is for some students rewarding is for most what Gifford has termed a "forced...diet of undergraduate education courses [necessary] for securing teaching credentials."[97] As a matter of some urgency, this sequence needs to be made much more. In the second part of this book we look, in some detail, at how it can be. We shall find that the answer involves reforming far more than education courses themselves.

The remainder of the first part of the book examines issues that provide a context for our recommendations. Chapter Four explores two central questions: What, fundamentally, are the educational needs of teachers? And, in the broadest terms, what kinds of programs do they imply?

CHAPTER FOUR

A LIBERAL AND PROFESSIONAL EDUCATION

Those with some years in the field will have deep sympathy with a sentiment expressed by James Conant: "When someone writes or says that what we need today in the United States is to decide first what we mean by the word 'education,' a sense of distasteful weariness overtakes me. I feel as though I were starting to see a badly scratched film of a poor movie for the second or third time."[98] Yet the matter of goals cannot be set aside so easily. At some point one has to get back to first purposes, to ask what we really want to provide in the schools. What should be their guiding philosophy?

We want to propose that the proper business of the schools is liberal education. It is true that the term "liberal education" seldom figures in discussion of the public schools. Since the term is traditionally associated with colleges and universities, it may seem to some "elitist" in this context. Recently, however, a group of leading secondary and postsecondary educators convened by the Christian A. Johnson Endeavor Foundation's Educational Leadership Project has argued forcefully that liberal education is a highly appropriate concept for the secondary schools.[99] In subscribing to their position, we also want to extend it. Appropriately understood, liberal education has efficacy as a guiding philosophy even in the middle and lower grades. The engagement with

A widened emphasis on liberal learning
would be profoundly democratic,
because it would challenge all students
to discover what is possible for them

and attitude toward subject matter that defines liberal learning is something that good teachers foster, no matter what the age of their students. It is the essence of what our schools ought to provide.

A liberal education includes both the study of certain kinds of material and the mastery of certain kinds of skills. Many subjects outside the traditional liberal arts can be vehicles for liberal education—and those within can be taught illiberally. A liberal education cannot take place, however, without appropriate content. Engagement with core liberal arts subjects such as literature, history, science, and mathematics is essential both to a liberal education and to any education in the schools. So, too, are the mastery of certain essential skills, habits of mind, and ways of understanding. Any liberal education—any strong education in the schools—will, that is, use engagement with subject matter to develop the skills of literacy, communication, critical thinking, and numeracy and an understanding of science. It will develop historical consciousness, an appreciation of the arts, and a sense for issues of value. It will provide the international and multicultural perspectives that take students into worlds beyond their own. In the process, a liberal education will foster curiosity, a love for learning, and what John Dewey called the contin-

ued capacity for growth.

This catalogue suggests that although a liberal education includes mastery of "the basics" and foundation work in all the traditional fields of study, it aims still higher. Liberal education is the outcome of students becoming, in the Educational Leadership Project's phrase, "involved with content in a particular way": it develops precisely those "higher-order" skills—reasoning, critical thinking, synthesis, and the like—in which, according to the NAEP and other assessments, students in our schools are most deficient.[100]

There is no reason to think that the idea of liberal education is too "elitist" for the schools or inappropriate in any way to the growing population of at-risk students. A widened emphasis on liberal learning would be profoundly democratic, because it would challenge all students to discover what is possible for them. By nurturing capacities and values necessary for achievement, liberal education can be an especially effective antidote to the despair, frustrations, and feelings of hopelessness that can impede young people's progress and aspirations.[101] Lauren Resnick, Diane Ravitch, and others have argued persuasively that all students need to acquire the higher-order thinking skills fostered by a liberal education.[102]

No one denies the difficulty of

teaching the half of all youth who are now shunted off into non-academic courses of study. Such tracking, however, sells these students short. As Ravitch points out, many "non-college bound" students—indeed some who drop out—do go on to enroll in college five or ten years after their classmates.[103] Citing Michael Oakeshott, Donna Kerr nicely describes education as "an initiation into the human conversation, a process of understanding experience in the ways that humankind has invented."[104] If the goal of our schools is to produce individuals who as citizens, workers, and human beings can fully understand that conversation and participate in it, then we need to make liberal education a priority for all of them.

If liberal education is to be the focus of the schools, it follows not only that teaching professionals should be "liberal educators" but that they themselves should be both professionally and liberally educated. To explain and support this view, we draw on current thinking about what teachers need to know and be able to do. We shall find few reasons here for preferring the simple "liberal arts" or "teacher education" paradigms of teacher preparation. A more flexible and comprehensive conception is needed, one that integrates study in the liberal arts and in education. Only if prospective teach-

ers become—to paraphrase the Educational Leadership Project—involved with both kinds of content in a particular way can their preparation be at once liberal and professional and truly adequate to their—and society's—needs.

What must a teacher know and be able to do? The literature on education offers many answers—some thoughtful, some pat, some in the form of speciously systematic catalogues. The best of them, however, reveal a shared view of teaching as a complex and demanding activity. They agree broadly, as well, on the capacities and kinds of knowledge and understanding essential to classroom effectiveness.

Today's teachers have been described as "overtrained in pedagogy and undereducated in subject matter."[105] Yet the foundation of teacher effectiveness—and surely its larger part—is a knowledge of the subject matter and approaches of the liberal arts. While all professionals use such knowledge in their work, teaching is about knowledge.[106] It employs knowledge as its primary tool and forges it as its primary product. A broad and thorough knowledge of the liberal arts is therefore the central element of the profession's instrumental base.[107]

To acquire the knowledge they need, teachers must range across the entire university curriculum—more broadly, in fact, than students preparing for careers in medicine or the law.[108] At the same time, they have a particular need to know some of what they know in depth. We are beginning to realize that our time-honored distinctions between general education and academic specialty have not served us particularly well; they have brought us general education without depth or purpose and inward-looking concentrations absorbed with their own technical concerns. Nonetheless the two rubrics are useful in sorting out some of the key ways in which, for teachers, the liberal arts are important.

Teachers must be able to draw on a broad and rigorous general education. However that education is provided to them by colleges and universities, they need to have been introduced to all the principal domains of knowledge—including the humanities, social sciences, fine arts, mathematics, and natural sciences—and they need to have a broad, if basic, understanding of their content. Teachers also must have some feeling for the unique ways that a variety of key disciplines apprehend reality—their characteristic concerns, the questions they ask, the evidence they recognize, the procedures they employ. At the same time, teachers, above all others, need to have an integrated view of knowledge that can help students place what they learn

in "the big picture." So teachers need to have a well-developed sense of the connections among these different ways of knowing. Their understanding of the fields they have studied in their general education should be broad. But they should have had the experience of involvement and immersion in active enquiry, and they should be prepared to pursue further study—should they want or need to—on their own. A broad and rigorous general education is essential to the credibility and effectiveness of teachers not only in their classrooms, but also in their dealings with the world outside. As has often been noted, teachers will never win respect or be accorded true professional status until they are seen as exemplars of broad learning.[109]

Some teachers have no idea what it is to study something in depth, because they have never done so.[110] Yet an in-depth knowledge of one or more areas of the liberal arts also is essential to virtually every teacher. Elementary and secondary teachers alike need to have a degree of mastery in all fields that they teach—and a far more advanced understanding of them than their most able students. They need to know, for any discipline they teach, what it is "to be on the inside of...[these] form[s] of thought and awareness" and to have effective control over them.[111]

We can differentiate "the engagement with scholarship expected of those preparing for lives of academic specialization or research" from that expected of those preparing to teach in the schools.[112] The latter should understand, however, far more about their discipline than just the knowledge—the facts, concepts, and theories—it supplies. They should have a sure sense of the phenomena and objects it tries to explain, the arguments it makes, the questions it asks. They should be skilled in its modes of enquiry, the use of its tools, and the interpretation of its symbols; understand how the discipline organizes knowledge for study; know how its current knowledge was created; and comprehend how it gathers and validates new knowledge. More broadly, teachers need to be acquainted with the history and tradition of a field and with its philosophical presuppositions. They need to know what is important enough about a field to "merit deep study and [what is] merely interesting or trivial."[113] The effective teacher will have thought about the social and ethical implications, uses and abuses, and limits of any subject he or she teaches.

For teachers, studying a liberal arts field in depth also implies both special strength in those particular aspects of it most likely to be taught and sound preparation in cognate fields.[114] There are many discontinuities between the organization of instruction at the elementary, secondary, and college levels. As Robert Shoenberg reminds us, teachers need to "hold" their knowledge in ways consistent with the organization of high school and elementary curricula, not the graduate schools.[115] English majors who know little about composition, linguistics, art, or history; history majors who know little world history, geography, or religion; math majors who know little trigonometry, science, computing, or statistics; biology majors who know little chemistry, or are too narrowly trained to handle classes in earth science: teachers like these are all too common in the schools. The range of subjects in which they need depth notwithstanding, it is also important that teachers understand their specialty areas in an integrated way. Their knowledge should reflect not merely the accumulation of courses but a synthesis of their academic experiences. They need to have considered how various subject matters and approaches relate to one another—and to issues and concerns in the world at large.

Like a sound general education, this kind of in-depth understanding of their teaching fields will benefit teachers both in the classroom and outside it. As John Dewey observed, subject mastery is powerful precisely because it frees the teacher to attend

Effective teachers also need
an understanding of pedagogy
that is specific to discipline and content

to pupils.[116] Teachers will need to demonstrate these professional levels of subject mastery before they are extended professional autonomy.

Many in the arts and sciences think a strong general education and in-depth knowledge of some area in the liberal arts sufficient preparation for teaching. Some of these individuals regard good teaching as a knack of personality.[117] Others think that what study in the arts and sciences does not provide, common sense and experience can. Still others concede some theoretical value to formal training in pedagogy but dismiss out of hand the possibility of future teachers getting anything useful out of existing education courses.

It requires no defense of the status quo to argue that the well-prepared teacher will have studied pedagogy and other topics in education. All but the most solipsistic college teachers know how often what is taught is not learned. They know the limited value of either common sense or long experience in helping to overcome this problem. Yet college instructors have the advantage of teaching relatively few classes. Their students are both self-selected and relatively homogeneous in socio-economic background, preparation, ability, and motivation. Even if their students cannot all be assumed to have a strong interest in the subject, most can be counted on to be inter-

ested at least in completing their coursework with a good grade.

Teachers in the schools, on the other hand, generally teach many more students. They meet their students more often and on terms less conducive to learning. Those students, typically, also represent a much wider spectrum of background, readiness, interest, and aspiration. And they are, of course, younger—emotionally and intellectually at a far greater developmental remove from their teachers than undergraduates are from theirs.

Some elementary and secondary teachers prove to be gifted exceptions to the general rule that teachers need help with their teaching. Some have the luxury of teaching in settings (often suburban or private) that resemble college campuses more than most public schools. In a typical school, however—let alone one with more than its share of low achievers—effective teaching generally requires more than subject matter preparation, even of the highest quality. It is with pedagogical approaches that practicing teachers most often ask for help.[118] We might wish more were concerned with deepening their understanding of the subjects they teach, but it is clear that they need specifically instructional resources as well.

The first and broadest such resource is an understanding of the enterprise of education, as opposed more strictly to pedagogy or teaching methods. Why do we have schools? With what ends in mind do we educate our young? What is the history of education? What philosophies and social forces have animated it and clash for control of it today? The school, the family, the growing, learning child: each is a concept and a reality that teachers need to understand from a variety of perspectives. All teachers, regardless of the subjects they teach or the levels at which they teach, need to have learned about these fundamentals and grappled with the normative and moral issues they raise. In the process, all should have been both oriented to the profession and given critical perspectives upon it that will make them agents for change.[119]

Teachers also need, of course, to be informed and competent in a variety of areas bearing more directly upon classroom instruction. Several of these areas of pedagogical knowledge are generic, in large part specific neither to particular subjects nor to particular grade levels. They include classroom organization and management, observation and evaluation of student learning, the use of educational technologies, counseling of pupils and parents, and generic instructional strategies (drawn from both common wisdom and a growing research base).[120] Ef-

fective teachers, however, also need an understanding of pedagogy that is specific to discipline and content. "Learning one's subjects and learning to teach are not enough," Willis Hawley has noted. "Learning to teach one's subjects should be the goal."[121] One can only go so far answering the question, "How does one teach?" The real intellectual interest, and practically the far more important challenge, lies in answering questions such as, "How do I explain the binomial theorem, or the history of the slave trade, to junior high students? Teach astronomy to first graders? The subjunctive mood to eight graders? *King Lear* to an advanced literature class of high school seniors?"

The answers to these questions constitute what Lee Shulman has termed "pedagogical content knowledge"—the content one has to know in order to teach, as opposed to "telling what you know" and hoping for ignition.[122] Requiring a thorough grasp of specific subject matter, this kind of pedagogical knowledge tells one how students learn (or fail to learn) a given idea or technique and how, given their prior knowledge and preconceptions, they can be helped to do so. It puts at one's disposal—for a particular student engaging with a particular subject—explanations, analogies, and other representations that, in Frank Murray's phrase, "support the recon-figuration of what you know into something teachable."[123] It is know-ing that in explaining Newtonian mechanics, one can help students by suggesting that they think of the world as a system of billiard balls—and knowing how the analogy does and does not work. It is knowing that an initial discussion of rights is likely to founder on a confusion be-tween moral and legal rights, and that the case of blacks in the Repub-lic of South Africa (who have the one but few of the other) can clarify the difference. "I know what time is," said St. Augustine, "as long as no one asks me."[124] Teachers will be asked, and a subject-based pedagogy rather than general instructional technique is what can see them through.

In addition to knowing how to teach their subject, teachers should believe that it matters. To the stu-dent who asks "why we need to know polynomials, anyway," an ef-fective answer will not be, "so you'll know how to factor."[125] The case for grammar can't be hung on the likeli-hood of its inclusion on the SATs. A teacher has to have thought through and has to speak with conviction about connections with real life—and better still project a curiosity and zest for what is being taught that will bring it alive for others. To do this, teachers need to be active stu-dents themselves, lifelong learners who know their discipline as "an imaginative way of thinking, a disci-pline of intellectual love."[126] They need to present their field as some-thing they themselves are involved with and want to share, even—per-haps especially—with that 30 to 40 percent of students who see little to be gained from doing well in school and are "difficult" to teach.[127]

Similarly, teachers need to be able to engage their students in active modes of learning. Because student achievement correlates strongly with intensity of involvement, students need to know learning as a process, not a product—a verb, not a noun.[128] In studying history and science, stu-dents need to engage themselves in the process of what historians and scientists *do*—not simply be presented with their conclusions. There always will be a role for what Jerome Bruner has termed "expository" teaching, but teachers need more of-ten to embrace Bruner's "hypotheti-cal" mode of teaching.[129] Then they become coaches as much as teach-ers—collaborators who free their stu-dents from the dicta of authority in order to encourage and guide them in inductive, independent thinking.

Close collaboration with students can help teachers in meeting another important expectation: that they be active inquirers not only into their fields but also into the teaching and learning process. It is not coinciden-tal that recent reports emphasize the notion of the teacher as "thoughtful" professional.[130] Teachers need to be analytical and, in the best sense, self-conscious about their teaching. They also need to be skilled and systema-tic observers of the ways their stu-dents learn. Only if they routinely examine and reflect upon their expe-riences will they begin to develop an informed sense of the strengths and weaknesses of alternative modes of instruction and how—by student, by subject, by level of instruction—these approaches should be used. It is not enough for a teacher to live through the day, as considerable an accom-plishment as that can sometimes seem. He or she should be able to learn from it and become a better teacher the next day as a result.

Finally, we would like our teachers to have an integrated understanding of all the different parts of their edu-cation. Their sense of the connected-ness of things must go beyond even a mastery of pedagogical content knowledge. Their education will usu-ally be served up piecemeal, but teachers need to know how its topics are fitted to a whole. They must ap-preciate the place of theory in giving "a fact its meaning or a skill its rele-vance" yet, as professionals, concern themselves centrally with how theo-ry and fact play themselves out in practice.[131] Somehow, that is, they

must bring all the theories and facts, paradigms and practices together into something coherent, dynamic, and serviceable in the classroom. Whitehead writes of an "active wisdom."[132]

In sum, there is much that we want teachers to know and be able to do. We wish them to have a broad and deep command of liberal arts subject matter and an under-standing of the contexts and theories of education, of general pedagogy, and of the pedagogy demanded by specific students and subject matters. We expect them to teach with conta-gious interest and conviction, to ex-emplify active and collaborative learning, and to be thoughtful, cre-ative students themselves of teaching and learning. We want them, finally, to have made of their education something more than the sum of its parts. We want them to have come to understand all they have learned in an integrated, meaningful way that empowers and motivates them for their craft.

The education implied by these criteria must be a lifelong endeavor. It needs to be well begun before one teaches—but it cannot be completed in four, five, six, or seven years of study. It also cannot be an education that focuses on narrow, technical, or instrumental concerns—or, for that matter, solely on the subject matter of the traditional liberal arts.

The kind of education implied would be unusually broad and in large part both liberal and professional. It would provide general education, a liberal arts concentration, and professional education not separately from one another but as parts of an integrated, liberal whole. The entire education, finally, would be one that at every turn involves future teachers with the kind of active, collaborative, interdisciplinary, and reflective teaching and learning we want them to bring to the schools.

We turn next to the case that has been made for placing preservice teacher preparation programs at the graduate level. This review will suggest a number of reasons why, for most institutions, integrated baccalaureate-level programs represent a better alternative—one more in keeping with the ideals we have spelled out here.

CHAPTER FIVE

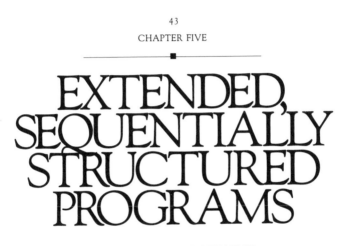

EXTENDED, SEQUENTIALLY STRUCTURED PROGRAMS

THE APPEAL OF AUTONOMY

ASSUMPTIONS AND CONSEQUENCES

The last few years have brought several proposals that teacher education be extended to five or more years. This chapter focuses on these five- and six-year proposals, because they raise clearly relevant issues of program length and structure. We review some of the professional context from which these proposals have arisen, question some of the assumptions on which they are based, and point out the possibility of unintended and unfortunate consequences.

Although the idea of extended programs was not original with either the Holmes Group of research universities or the Carnegie Forum on Education and the Economy, these organizations first brought it to national prominence in their 1986 reports *Tomorrow's Teachers* and *A Nation Prepared: Teachers for the 21st Century*, respectively. The two reports differ in their emphases; both propose eliminating the undergraduate major in teacher education and moving professional education to the graduate level. These graduate-level

Colleges and universities will need
to provide...the option of completing
both arts and sciences majors
and certification requirements
within four years

---

programs then would require an undergraduate degree in the arts and sciences for admission.

Much of the early response to the Holmes proposal urged that the nation consider the source: a group of research universities whose schools of education by their own admission have a long history of deemphasizing teacher preparation in the interests of specialized education research. Now these same education schools, it was said, had seen an opportunity to increase their enrollments by cornering the market on teacher education and to bolster their low status on their own campuses in the process.[133] The partisan nature of the response perhaps was understandable in light of early references by the Holmes leadership to taking the teaching of teachers away from "second-class...that is...undergraduate faculty [and] reduc[ing] the number of institutions [that educate teachers] over time."[134]

Subsequent statements from the Holmes Group reveal more modesty about its members' aspirations in teacher education and stress that its members wish to eliminate four-year programs only at their own institutions. They point out that, to the extent that research and development are central to teacher education reform, the research universities have a key role to play.[135] More importantly, partly under pressure from

its membership, the Holmes Group has softened its emphasis on a sequential model that would place work in the arts and sciences before work in teacher education. It first allowed for the possibility of a few "pre-education" courses at the undergraduate level.[136] More recently it has become clear that many of the group's member institutions are working to build into their programs a higher degree of integration. The Holmes Group has held to its vision of an extended course of study, however, and still would expect beginning Holmes graduates to be given a higher rung than other novices on any career ladder.[137]

The Carnegie report, on the other hand, is as much a political as an educational document, responding to problems of international competitiveness with prescriptions of a range of economically useful literacies.[138] As with the Holmes report, the quality of its analysis is high, and many of its recommendations are on target. The Carnegie report's most important contribution may be its call for a National Board of Professional Teaching Standards. This entity, which recently has been organized, will issue certificates to teachers who demonstrate high levels of professional expertise. It might in time lift the expectations of credentialing agencies and employing school systems nationwide.

The Carnegie report joined the Holmes report in calling for extended teacher preparation. It seemed to some, however, to do so without much conviction or reason. Because its emphasis was on a mechanism for assessing teachers "however...prepared," the report's own logic argued for openness to different ways of preparing them.[139]

Although the Holmes and Carnegie reports need to be understood in relation to the two groups' auspices, they did bring teacher education into prominence as an issue of national concern. And even though the former report seems not to reflect accurately the Holmes Group's current very constructive agenda, both reports continue strongly to influence thinking about institutional options. Indeed, the ideas they present with respect to the length and structure of teacher education programs have had the effect of crowding out consideration of other models of reform. This is unfortunate, for although the reports are seminal and useful documents, their recommendations point a direction for reform opposite to that which most institutions probably should pursue. Multiple paths into the profession will increase the numbers of highly qualified entrants, and preservice graduate-level professional programs are highly appropriate for some prospective teachers and insti-

tutions. As we shall argue, however, if significant numbers of arts and sciences students are to be attracted to teaching and prepared for it in ways that will develop in them the qualities we want our teachers to have, colleges and universities generally will need to provide two things: the option of completing both arts and sciences majors and certification requirements within four years and challenging, richly integrated programs in which to do so.

THE APPEAL OF AUTONOMY

In 1986, when the major proposals to extend teacher education were first published, some characterized them as expressing a "consensus" in the field and confidently predicted that in a short time "almost everybody" would be considering the five-year model.[140] In fact, the proposals enjoy limited support. Recent surveys show that they have many more advocates in larger universities than elsewhere.[141] Even land-grant institutions divide on the proposals' merits, however, and the recommendations have little currency in other settings.[142] The backing they do have, however, derives in part from the fact that they accommodate a desire of some, if by no means most, teacher educators to separate teacher education programs from the liberal arts and/or make them more specialized. This factor in the current discussions about preparing teachers is not well understood by those outside of teacher education and is worth looking at a bit more closely.

Teacher educators are understandably frustrated by the view, widely held in the academy, "that there is no substance to [their field], at least not independent of a thorough... knowledge of subject matter."[143] Some, including many advocates of extended programs, therefore argue that the primary means of ensuring the legitimacy of their discipline is to reorient it thoroughly around a distinctive "knowledge base" drawn from educational research. There are references to an assumed "science of teaching."[144]

The majority of teacher educators, however, seem not to subscribe to the idea that educational research, programmatic autonomy, or separate graduate status are solutions to the problems of the field. Most do strongly support a variety of promising efforts to identify, synthesize, and make more central in their programs a body of specifically professional knowledge.[145] They see this knowledge coming, however, from the sophisticated "lore of successful practice" as well as from an empirical research base.[146] (One critic has termed the claims made for the latter "vague" and "extravagant.")[147] Many are concerned that while re-

ports like those of Holmes and Carnegie speak persuasively of the value of a liberal arts education, these reports' authors seem to have treated this as something to be acquired before getting down to the real business of professional education.

Teacher educators do not divide on these issues simply according to whether their own programs are undergraduate or graduate. Some of the strongest (and most unvarnished) expressions of a wish to free teacher education from association with the undergraduate liberal arts curriculum come from advocates of the undergraduate major in teacher education. "The best accommodation between liberal and professional education must be based upon mutual exclusivity," writes an undergraduate education dean in a recent issue of the *Journal of Teacher Education.* "Otherwise the two domains confuse themselves and each other about their respective purposes.... We ought to leave the liberal education of teachers up to our colleagues in the arts and sciences.... It is equally important to exclude liberal arts faculty, in general, from direct involvement in teacher education."[148]

One can disagree with some teacher educators' visions of a much more specialized, freestanding discipline and the steps by which they would establish it on either the graduate or undergraduate level, yet still feel some sympathy for their efforts. Teacher educators are dedicated professionals, yet their field, as Dennis O'Brien has put it, is "not the path to academic preferment."[149] It is a relatively low-cost but underfunded enterprise that many colleges and universities engage in only because historically it has generated more revenue than it has consumed and provided programs in which large numbers of average and below-average students could be enrolled.[150] In some settings it is regulated to within an inch of its life. Teacher education faculty members are held generally accountable for the overall preparation of students who do between 50 and 80 percent of their coursework with liberal arts faculty members. They put up with the latter's suspicions and sometimes outright dismissal of "the legitimacy of their work, the quality of their students, and the intellectual rigor of their programs," but they seldom enjoy their colleagues' cooperation or support.[151]

Faculty members in education have problems paralleling those of teachers in the schools: low pay, low status, and poor working conditions.[152] Serving both their institutions and their public constituencies, they are in many respects not of the campus in the same sense as other faculty. Because, traditionally, three-quarters of teacher educators have

begun their careers in the elementary and secondary schools, some have difficulty in adjusting to the norms of higher education.[153] Teacher educators work within the same research and publication-prizing reward system as faculty members in other disciplines. Yet, having "an extremely low record of scholarly accomplishment" due at least in part to heavy demands for involvements in clinical settings, they seem sometimes to fall farther and farther behind.[154] It is no wonder that many within the field want to change things radically, some by establishing teacher education on the same graduate-level footing as professional programs in medicine or law.

A move to graduate status makes a certain kind of sense for teacher education because of the sociology of the professions and the academic disciplines. "A review of the evolution of several professions," writes one proponent, "demonstrates that increases in salary and social esteem are preceded by increases in the duration and level of professional preparation."[155] This has certainly been the case with business education, which is perhaps a better analogy on several counts than law or medicine. On the other hand, the specialized and research-oriented MBA programs that made business schools reputable also may have made them less effective in producing good all-around managers. Proposals for educational reform must be judged ultimately by their ability to improve the education of students. To the degree that proposals for extended and sequential programs might fall short by this measure, we need to find other means of addressing the legitimate problems facing teacher education as a profession.

ASSUMPTIONS AND CONSEQUENCES

Some maintain that there are compelling educational reasons for moving to a curriculum that is five or six years in length. "The curriculum must be extended," according to one leading teacher educator, "for if we try to squeeze more into the present four-year period we would have to compromise something essential—either the general-liberal studies, the sound mastery of the subjects to be taught, or the professional studies themselves. If we are going to have a professional, well-educated teacher... the full program of training must be elongated."[156] This argument has had its champions for at least thirty years. However, it is only as good as its assumptions: that we can have a first-rate education for teachers where we provide its parts in separation from each other; that time spent studying a subject tends to be the key to how well it is learned; and that time given to one subject is time lost to another.

These assumptions may reflect a limited view of what a curriculum can and ought to be. Certainly they underestimate the opportunities at our disposal to improve what is offered within a four-year baccalaureate framework. They tolerate and, in fact, reinforce the current schism between liberal and professional education.[157] They overlook not only how much time can be "recovered" by the elimination of unnecessary or redundant content but also how much is to be gained by articulating and integrating the different parts of a student's course of study.

We can do far more with the time available. There never seems to be enough time for any curriculum so long as we think in terms of different kinds of subject matter competing for inclusion within it. The issue, however, is not the claims of the liberal arts versus those of professional education; it is how the two fields of study can be pulled together into a more powerful whole. In this respect, "the usual more/less, longer/shorter... quantitative" cast of earlier reform proposals does not serve us well.[158] We need to think not about adding more courses, but about making the ones we offer more educative.

Fortunately, single autonomous programs and courses are not the only imaginable units of curricular organization.[159] Curricular change can, of course, move such units around, prefer some over others, or—failing all else—simply add more units to the whole. But reforming the education of teachers requires a subtler and more searching process. Figuratively, it requires looking within units to identify essential content and ask how its delivery as a whole can be strengthened. In some cases this may mean adding courses. Often, however, by eliminating overlap and the inessential, by linking treatments across courses, by adding new dimensions to existing courses—in short, by both pruning the curriculum and enriching and coordinating its content—more can be accomplished with less.

In fact, the most serious problem with proposals like those of the original Holmes and Carnegie reports is that by arguing that liberal arts preparation should precede professional education, such proposals discourage their integration. Not only is integration what makes a four-year curriculum for future teachers possible, it is—as the Holmes Group itself now stresses—also an important source of strength for any program.

The typical case in higher education, unfortunately, is the college or university in which professors attend only to their own courses, addressing their respective subject matters in unconnected and often competing ways. While the traditional autonomy afforded faculty members has produced many excellent courses, it has not necessarily led to coherent programs.[160] Participating faculty members have been surprised and dismayed by evidence from recent assessment research showing that students compartmentalize what they have learned in different courses or even at different points in the same course, failing to put it together unless they are encouraged and shown how to do so.[161]

In recent years, increasing numbers of institutions have established, and seen for themselves the advantages of, integrative, interdisciplinary curricula.[162] Research shows that courses of study that encourage students to integrate ideas and skills produce the greatest growth in critical thinking.[163] They seem to foster contextual understanding and—as one set of disciplinary values and approaches is challenged and enriched by another—reflection and intellectual synthesis.

These are general arguments for integrative study. Our earlier review of the qualities we expect of teachers implies other reasons specific to teacher education and the liberal arts. As we have seen, teachers have a special need for an integrated understanding of their general education, of the knowledge they will teach, of education and pedagogy, and of the relations among all these areas.

A sequentially structured course of study would do little to give them this. It treats knowledge of the arts and sciences as preparatory to professional study, not as "central to the daily performance of classroom teaching."[164] Even now, when in most settings professional education and liberal arts courses both are taken at the undergraduate level, the curriculum lacks connectedness. Prospective teachers—whether liberal arts majors or education majors—often travel a lonely and discontinuous route back and forth between the two realms. They are left largely on their own to relate their study of, say, the psychology and sociology of human learning to their knowledge of math or history.[165]

Serially structured programs would only worsen this problem. There would be little hope of merging the consideration of subject matter and how to teach it in programs that do not allow students to encounter these components of a teacher's education simultaneously. It is not enough, however, to preserve undergraduate formats; we must realize their potential for integration. Only if we do can four-year programs be more effective than those of any other type—including longer, sequentially structured ones in which students at least have the advantage of spending more time on task.

This last point brings us, finally and briefly, to another likely consequence of extended, sequentially structured programs: a counterproductive effect on recruiting. Making extended programs of five or six years' length the standard route into teaching would be enormously expensive. Even if the increased costs to students were partially offset by scholarships and loans—and it is by no means clear who would foot the bill—economic disincentives would remain.

The new proposals also make little or no provision for giving large numbers of undergraduate liberal arts majors the kinds of formal exposure to education as a profession and field of study that might lead them to pursue a graduate degree in the field. The expectation, of course, is that once programs are extended, students who are now education majors would be arts and sciences majors; but many of them might not be willing to put off their professional education until graduate school.

A worrisome prospect comes into focus when we consider these facts together: a possible combination of increased costs and lowered student interest that would ensure a loss of students to the profession. Of special concern, too, is the likelihood that increased costs would hit those with low incomes hardest. Many of these would be minority students—the black and Hispanic teachers we need most critically in the schools.[166]

We have found in this chapter few reasons to support the widespread development of extended, sequentially structured programs and some for actively resisting it. In Chapter Six we consider some of the reasons why, despite its advantages, the alternative of creating well-integrated baccalaureate-level programs for arts and sciences majors has not been widely tried. We focus on what is certainly the greatest obstacle—the values and attitudes of arts and sciences faculty members—and suggest lines along which these attitudes need to be rethought.

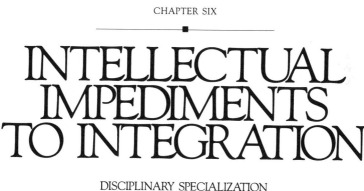

INTELLECTUAL IMPEDIMENTS TO INTEGRATION

DISCIPLINARY SPECIALIZATION

A NEW RATIONALE FOR INVOLVEMENT

Merle Borrowman once observed that one cannot "overstate the propensity of speculative minds to lose all perception of reality nor the tendency of practitioners to lose their perception of possibility."[167] With this wisdom in mind, in this chapter we want to acknowledge and comment on some key impediments to the development of four-year integrated programs of teacher preparation for arts and sciences majors. Rooted as they are in the dominant culture and value systems of higher education, these obstacles are real. They tend, however, to be intellectual, not political or financial, obstacles. We

need most of all to think harder about what we do.

The University of Georgia system recently has made a major effort to improve the education of teachers. With state support, colleges are forming regional centers to work with local schools. What is learned is being put back in the college classroom to produce better teachers. The system's experience with this exemplary initiative is instructive. While the state's colleges have worked together readily and the colleges and school districts have forged productive partnerships, a third kind of cooperation has proved much more difficult to

The major resistance to cooperation is not
from teacher educators who wish
to establish their field as more
of a freestanding discipline; it comes
overwhelmingly from within the liberal arts

achieve: cooperation among faculty members from different areas of the same institution. According to one account, "relations between faculties of education and liberal arts units are often strained or nonexistent."[168] This common problem is the chief impediment to progress in improving the college preparation of teachers. The major resistance to cooperation is not from teacher educators who wish to establish their field as more of a freestanding discipline; it comes overwhelmingly from within the liberal arts. The reasons are worth examining.

DISCIPLINARY SPECIALIZATION

As David Perkins recently observed, "There is hardly a university in the country where reputation, promotion, and salary do not depend primarily or exclusively on publications and on other [research-related] activities."[169] This emphasis on research in assessing faculty is by no means limited to universities. It is long established at what David Reisman calls the "research colleges," and to varying degrees it has taken hold in the last two decades in virtually all institutions—including the former teachers colleges.

Reward systems emphasizing research have had the intended effect of increasing specialization and publication and, at some places, of

bringing to sponsoring institutions the prestige and money that often attends such work. Because it is the disciplines that organize and validate specialized research, the principal loyalty of many faculty members now is to their fields and their fellow practitioners. As Ernest Boyer reports, most faculty members identify first with their disciplinary guilds, second with their departments, and only third with the colleges and universities in which they work.[170]

There is much about higher education that perpetuates this situation. The professoriat, for example, comes predominantly from the kinds of undergraduate and graduate institutions that most emphasize specialization. Few of these institutions include any formal consideration of the larger responsibilities of college teaching in the training of future faculty members. Our institutions organize themselves into schools and departments, and in the political economy of most institutions these "adept protectors and advocates of [disciplinary] interests" wield considerable control over the allocation of resources.[171] Even when professors organize themselves beyond the campus it is in most cases not as teachers but "as intellectuals and guardians of their disciplines."[172]

Disciplinary specialization is essential to the pursuit of advanced knowledge. It has brought countless benefits to society and to higher education, and, under proper conditions, it supports and inspires good teaching. As many national reports have argued, however, too often it has tended to weaken our undergraduate programs. At some institutions the greater glory of graduate education and the headlong rush into a world of megagrants, high technology research parks, and profitable joint ventures have made the undergraduate experience little more than an inconvenient afterthought. More typical are colleges and universities that recognize undergraduate education as an important mission but give it little help in the competition for faculty time and effort. The challenge, of course, is to find ways to preserve and strengthen our institutions as centers for the creation of new knowledge while renewing their integrity and vitality as providers of high-quality undergraduate instruction.

Unchecked faculty specialization can enervate the undergraduate enterprise—and impede cooperation in the education of teachers—in numerous ways, but four deserve special mention. First, the institutional overestimation of research can diminish the perceived importance of teaching and therefore the effort that faculty members put into it. "In the university," Harriet Sheridan has written, "concerns about teaching are generally regarded as the second-best preoccupation of those who have not been successful in the world of scholarship."[173] Although teaching is the first business of undergraduate programs in any setting, faculty members everywhere speak revealingly of "teaching *loads* and research *opportunities*, never the reverse."[174]

Many faculty members do take their teaching seriously and work hard at it, but for too many others teaching is a duty that can be discharged with clear and logical presentations.[175] Those students fortunate enough to understand do; the rest may be left behind. In other words, the attention of college faculty members is, as it should be, on their material, but it is not enough—where it also should be—on the learner.

Although faculty members are impressively strong on content, many are ignorant of the different ways in which humans think and learn and the developmental stages through which their students pass during their college years. Having given little serious thought to the kinds of difficulty students might have in understanding what they present, faculty members tend to have but "one arrow in their quiver of [pedagogical] techniques."[176] Many would think it inappropriate to learn more about developmental stages, learning styles, and teaching strategies—or, for that matter, to give more time to the classroom. Moreover, they could accurately claim that they are not being paid to do that.

A second effect of specialization is that too frequently it discourages a concern with courses other than one's own and thus tends to fragment the undergraduate curriculum. The norms of higher education dictate a healthy and proper respect for the autonomy of what one does in one's own classroom. Because they are trained as specialists, however, faculty members often have little interest in making connections between their own courses and those of colleagues either within or beyond their departments. Some have an understandable fear of their own ignorance outside their field and see considerable risk in collaboration. Nor are these the only disincentives. Learning a new area is likely to claim time needed for research. Developing new courses or adapting old ones also may require released time, and interdisciplinary proposals often compete poorly with others that are more narrowly drawn. Finally, just as there is little recognition within one's specialty for work done outside it, there usually is little enthusiasm within one's department for faculty effort expended elsewhere. The situation recalls Erasmus's comparison of the fox and the hedgehog. In the modern university, the fox—who

knows many things—might be good for the undergraduate curriculum. The hedgehog—who knows one thing very well—has the advantage for promotion and tenure.

Third, specialization can discourage appropriate professional involvements with society at large. As Merrill D. Peterson points out, public outreach was not part of the conception of the modern American university.[177] If research, teaching, and service are the concerns of tenure and promotion committees, there is little doubt which is the least of these, especially if it is rendered off campus. Service ranks even below teaching, and in the university, where many professional faculty members must maintain close relations with the field, it is valued least by the arts and sciences.[178] The result too often is that while talent and effort are lavished on certain kinds of needs, they are denied to others which may be equally, or even more, important. "The ablest people we have in every field," argues John Gardner, "must give thought to the largest problems of the nation. They don't have to be in government to do so, but they do have to come out of the trenches of their own specialty and look at the whole battlefield."[179] Harlan Cleveland makes the same point with still harder words: "American higher education, which ought to be focusing on larger, urgent issues, is mired in disciplinary self-indulgence."[180]

Fourth, the preeminence of disciplinarity in the academy's value system ensures that education as a field of study is held in particularly low regard. The sophistication and validity of this field's knowledge base has been at issue since it began to claim a place in the universities at the turn of the century. The field often has tried to distance itself from its origins in the normal schools, which typically emphasized the "how" of teaching over the "what" or "why"; yet these very efforts sometimes have contributed to the impression that it is not a true discipline.[181] Education is a pseudo-discipline, writes one critic, "that uses jargon and studiedly unintelligible writing to restate the obvious, [and] dresses the art of teaching in the trappings of 'science,' producing much that is faddish and almost nothing that is useful."[182] This is a particularly dyspeptic expression of a view that is widely held: that education is an "amalgam of borrowed concepts from field experience, the social sciences and a smattering of conventional wisdom...supported only partially by empirical research," and that it serves essentially "to make the ordinary esoteric."[183]

It is abundantly clear from this review that integrative efforts between the liberal arts and teacher education start with numerous strikes against them. These efforts ask arts and sciences disciplinarians to collaborate across fields with what is to many of them a suspect discipline: education. They ask faculty members to develop interdisciplinary undergraduate curricula addressing, of all things, issues of teaching and learning. And they ask faculty members to do so largely in service to the schools. Put this way, the task of achieving truly integrative curricula might seem impossible. It clearly is, in some respects, the work of lifetimes.

One need not have illusions about the problem, however, to think that it can be dealt with. Strategies are available and progress can be made. The key, as always, is to give people reasons to change.

John Goodlad once summed up the challenge nicely: arts and sciences faculty members are skeptical that their involvement with prospective teachers and teacher education is appropriate, and they are in any event not rewarded for these efforts.[184] This formulation suggests the two broad fronts along which the battle for their support and participation needs to be waged. Among our suggestions in the second part of this book will be changes in the reward system that can give liberal arts faculty members incentives to undertake the effort—and perhaps risk—of becoming involved in the education

Faculty members need to understand their deep community of interest with teachers in the schools

of teachers. But we want to address briefly here the intellectual issue. Why *should* liberal arts faculty get involved? How is it appropriate or important for them as arts and sciences educators to do so?

A NEW RATIONALE FOR INVOLVEMENT

Faculty members need to understand their deep community of interest with teachers in the schools. The traditional hierarchy has valued teachers in proportion to the ages of the students they teach.[185] The traditional faculty attitude toward the failures of the schools has been that "they" have not been doing "their" job. As the interdependence—the essential unity—of our system of education has in recent years become more apparent, however, these hierarchies and assumptions have begun to some degree to be challenged. "We have met the enemy," Pogo says, "and he is us." Liberal arts faculty members need see that they themselves are an important part of the problems of the public schools.[186] Too often their own incoherent programs, desultory teaching, and refusal to be bothered with teaching their fields with any attention to the needs of prospective teachers bear a considerable share of the blame for sending unprepared teachers into the public schools' classrooms.

The effects of this inattention to teacher education work their destructive way through the entire system. Ironically, they are felt in time even by faculty members themselves. Because newly graduated teachers have such a poor grasp of the subjects they must teach, the schools in many cases have abandoned any serious effort to teach those subjects well. The students who graduate from the schools, in turn, present themselves to the colleges unprepared and often without any curiosity or real sense of what learning is. They naturally avoid the arts and sciences—to the great ambivalence of liberal arts faculty members. For although the latter still prefer not to be bothered, they do fret over falling enrollments and wonder how the general quality of the students coming out of the schools could ever have fallen so low.[187] "What happens—and what doesn't happen—in higher education has a strong and often deadening impact on the schools," wrote Don Davies twenty years ago. "The reverse is also true. Both higher and 'lower' education continue to poison each other's wells; in fact, it turns out to be a common well."[188]

Just as arts and sciences faculty members are part of the problem and inevitably among its victims, however, they also are among those who can best contribute to and benefit from its solution. In time they stand to get stronger students. There are, however, more important—and again, educational—considerations. Faculty members who recognize and act on their responsibility to help teach teachers will discover a profound complementarity between education as a professional field of study and the liberal arts.

Although there can be real value and appeal in aimless and unfocused study, there is the danger of futility, too. Professors in the arts and sciences know the frustration of teaching undergraduates whose work is not purposeful, yet many have seen students become consumed with a subject once they have discovered its connection to some larger purpose in their lives. Strong professional coursework can help give students' work in the arts and sciences point and direction as they discover its application and meaning in the larger world.[189] Future teachers' study of education can do even more. It can help them synthesize what they learn in the liberal arts and promote that additional reflection on it that fosters real understanding.[190]

The best education coursework, however, does not so much accompany or support serious study in the liberal arts as it does, in a sense, fulfill it. The integrated liberal-professional course of study asks students to think at every turn about how they might teach what they know to others. In Russell Edgerton's incisive phrase, it "conceives of teaching as an extension of knowing."[191] That conception, as Edgerton has pointed out, has a power to strengthen all our programs.

It may be that the highest calling is to teach our students so well that they can turn around and teach someone else. It turns out... that this is exactly what the degrees we give were originally intended to mean. If you go back to the history of the Italian university, "bachelor" is essentially an apprentice teacher. The word "master" means master teacher.[192] Long before our earliest universities existed, Edgerton adds, Aristotle argued "that the highest standard against which to measure whether an individual knows his subject matter is whether he can teach it to someone else."[193]

Charles Silberman has succinctly summarized these points about the complementarity of the two areas of study. "The most direct and immediate way of finding out what it is one really knows and how it can be applied—of finding the purpose and testing the human relevance of what one has learned—is to teach it to someone else." In this sense, he says, "teaching is the ultimate liberal art."[194] This may be the essential intellectual case for arts and sciences involvement—the rationale to which faculty members need to be educated. By helping their students become teachers, liberal arts faculty members are in no sense deviating from the aims of their disciplines. In fact, they are being radically true to those goals and holding students to their highest standards.

In this light, finally, all in higher education may want to be more thoughtful about assessing education's legitimacy and importance by conventional disciplinary measures. Perhaps, as some educationists contend, their field is a "young" discipline. Its claim to full disciplinary legitimacy may be made good in time. It seems to us, however, more fruitful to think of education rather as a special field of study and research. It is uniquely academic and professional—charged, at its best, with a productive tension between the claims of scholarship and practice.[195] In addition, it is more cross-disciplinary than other fields, drawing deeply and broadly on a wide variety of disciplines and making much of its contribution in its synthesis and extension of the understanding they provide. This is not a diminishing vision of education. It is one that makes clear how much of real importance the field's practitioners bring to the table and how important a place they deserve there.

■

RECOMMENDATIONS

A ROLE FOR INSTITUTIONAL LEADERS

STRENGTHENING THE INSTITUTION
AS AN ENVIRONMENT FOR TEACHING AND LEARNING

ADMINISTRATIVE STRUCTURES AND STRATEGIES

GENERAL EDUCATION AND LIBERAL ARTS ELECTIVES

STUDY IN THE MAJOR

STUDY IN PROFESSIONAL EDUCATION

THE ROLE OF THE STATES

How can a college or university recruit arts and sciences majors to teaching? How can it improve and integrate their general education, study of their major field, and study of education and pedagogy? How can it provide them, within a four-year baccalaureate program, the background they need in order to be recommended for certification?

The diversity of American higher education allows for few across-the-board prescriptions. More than twelve hundred colleges and universities offer degree and/or certification programs for future teachers; no other single professional curriculum is as widely offered.[196] These institutions represent the full spectrum of institutional types. Each type has its characteristic purposes, structure, and culture and its attendant strengths and weaknesses as a setting for the undergraduate education of teachers.

Land-grant and research universities, for example, often have strong faculties and selective student bodies. They are settings for sophisticated academic inquiry. They tend to have schools of education and to concentrate on graduate-level preparation of school administrators and various kinds of educational specialists rather than classroom teachers. These

Reform must begin…by working with the culture, structures, and personnel already in place

institutions often provide a poor climate for teacher preparation. Undergraduates considering teaching may be as likely to hear from their professors that they are too bright for that career as they are to be encouraged in pursuing it.[197]

Regional state colleges and universities play by far the largest role in teacher training.[198] Many were formerly normal schools and then teachers colleges themselves. They are sometimes judged to be high-volume, low-quality producers of teachers.[199] Their arts and sciences faculties, however, often take seriously a responsibility for teaching teachers, and structural arrangements may be more hospitable to cross-departmental study. Nonetheless, as some of these institutions have themselves embraced more of a research mission and adjusted their reward systems accordingly, internal division over the commitment to the teaching of teachers has become more common.[200]

Liberal arts colleges, like those of each institutional type, vary widely in quality. They include, however, many selective institutions. They are more likely than larger institutions to organize teacher education as a department (which may or may not offer a major) rather than as a separate school, and their education faculties often are stretched very thin; they sometimes have difficulty satis-

fying external agencies that they can mount sufficiently broad-based programs. The small size of these institutions, however, gives their education units some advantage in integrating their offerings with those of other disciplines. In many cases their faculties also exemplify a particularly strong commitment to teaching and the values that underlie it.

Given these institutional differences, we will not try to recommend for all campuses any one program or specific set of courses. Reform must begin in most cases by working with the culture, structures, and personnel already in place, and because the character of these varies so widely, different institutions will need different strategies. It is possible, however, to suggest what some of these will be. "I seen my opportunities," said the Tammany Hall ward heeler George Washington Plunkitt, "and I took 'em."

A ROLE FOR INSTITUTIONAL LEADERS

Most colleges and universities should begin from a common point—a decision either to take seriously the preparation of arts and sciences majors for teaching or not to undertake it at all. It has been the fate of conventional teacher education to exist in many institutions as "a second-rate subject, tolerated in principle but rarely supported with pride."[201] Although there might be less uneasiness with integrated programs preparing arts and sciences majors, institutions should face honestly and realistically the question of whether they are prepared to give such programs the support that they require. Few institutions are under any absolute obligation to prepare teachers by this route or any other.[202] Those who decide to do so, however, have a responsibility to do it well.

The highest officials of a college or university need to lead any reconsideration of the place of teacher preparation on the campus. College presidents, for the most part, have not been involved in the efforts of their institutions to improve the education of teachers.[203] Their failure to provide leadership goes far toward explaining how little progress has been made. Top institutional leaders have the attention of all who would have a part in making teacher preparation a college- or university-wide function. They have the command of resources to restructure incentives and encourage all the needed kinds of change. If they are seen as supporting consideration of a new initiative, the chances are good that it will be taken seriously—instead of as something that, if ignored, can be counted upon to go away.

While presidents, academic vice presidents, and other top academic leaders are assured of their colleagues' attention, their effectiveness in achieving lasting change will depend on their ability to persuade others to take ownership of reform. These leaders need to articulate a vision of change to which all can subscribe—a compelling rationale for their institution's involvement and a clear explanation of how proposed changes will serve the institution's mission and the interests of the faculty. They need to exemplify the cooperative and collaborative spirit in which the work must be carried out. They need to work closely with deans and faculty members, defining problems broadly and inviting involvement in the search for solutions. Their goals should be to empower others to oversee continuing change. If the goal is reforms that are meaningful and not merely cosmetic, however, they should expect to stay personally involved, lending the effort the visibility and continuing support that only they can provide.[204]

STRENGTHENING THE INSTITUTION AS AN ENVIRONMENT FOR TEACHING AND LEARNING

Institutions committing themselves to improving the preparation of liberal arts majors for teaching will have a common first challenge:

strengthening the entire campus as an environment for teaching and learning. We mean by this something larger than building or strengthening the particular curricular pathways that arts and sciences majors preparing to teach will travel. We mean making an intensified commitment to undergraduate education as a process that centers on learning and working to improve the institution comprehensively as a setting in which liberal learning thrives.

When new college graduates enter teaching, they have completed what Dan Lortie has termed "a seventeen-year apprenticeship of observation."[205] The first thirteen of those years typically have given them a sustained exposure to the practices that now inhibit learning in the schools. Too often, what has followed has done little to lift the student's sights: a final four years of exposure to college or university faculty members who neither take teaching very seriously nor, on average, do it particularly well. The prevailing practices are so strongly impressed upon students in their school and college years that even aggressive efforts to foster better pedagogical approaches fail. New and better approaches may be "learned," but then not even survive practice teaching.[206]

It has been said that how we teach is what we teach.[207] In that sense,

the proposals we review next show how the whole undergraduate experience can be transformed so that it reeducates students coming out of the schools and serves rather than subverts the education of aspiring teachers.

There is a rich literature on revitalizing undergraduate education. Commentators like Joseph Katz, Ernest Boyer, Zelda Gamson, and Frederick Rudolph have challenged higher education with their critiques of the undergraduate experience and visions of what it can be. Their work is seldom referred to in the voluminous literature on school and teacher education reform. Yet it has important implications for teacher preparation. It shows us the prospect of undergraduate environments transformed by new faculty attention to versatile and effective teaching and active, integrative learning—ideal settings in which to develop future teachers. Before turning specifically to integrated programs for liberal arts majors aspiring to teach, we review in this section key ideas emerging from this more general literature. These have to do with a range of topics: the study and assessment of teaching and learning, the use of active and experiential learning, the strengthening of academic advising, and the promotion of interdisciplinarity and curricular coherence.

Studying and assessing teaching and learning

"The overriding issue," Rudolph Weingartner has observed of undergraduate reform, "is the status and recognition of teaching" on campus.[208] Institutional leaders need to reassert the centrality of teaching. To do this is not to argue that research needs to be displaced as an important mission. It is merely to recognize that at any institution that prepares undergraduates, teaching must be valued equally and supported aggressively.[209]

Those who make this case may find unexpected support from the ranks of the faculty. According to Ernest Boyer, for example, 63 percent of all faculty members report that their interests lie more toward teaching than research. Even at research universities, 40 percent feel the same way. Moreover, more than half of faculty members at each type of institution agree that "teaching effectiveness, not publication, should be the primary criterion for promotion."[210] It is the reward system at least as much as any native faculty disposition that puts such a premium on publication—a fact that should come as good news to institutional leaders who favor reform and are in positions themselves to modify incentives.

Academic leaders can take a number of steps to strengthen undergraduate teaching. Numerous colleges and universities give awards for outstanding teaching at the undergraduate level. This form of recognition "[improves] faculty morale, collegiality, economic status and institutional commitment."[211] A few institutions have endowed distinguished teaching professorships. To various degrees, of course, many already take teaching into account in promotion and tenure decisions. Moving forward, however, will require recognizing that faculty members—in Weingartner's words again—"need to learn new things."[212] It also will require helping them to do so.

Among the most imaginative responses to this need are the growing numbers of campus centers (typically styled centers of "teaching and learning" and "instructional development") and departmentally based programs that provide interested faculty members and graduate students with assistance in becoming more effective classroom teachers. Institutions offering this kind of help include Harvard, Cornell, Northwestern, Stanford, Syracuse, Iowa State, Washington, and Brown universities and the universities of Chicago, Connecticut, and Georgia.[213]

Other institutions have had success in involving faculty in teaching workshops. The Central Pennsylvania Consortium, consisting of Dickinson, Franklin and Marshall, and

Gettysburg colleges, has found, for example, that participants in its annual faculty-led workshops "relish the time spent talking seriously about teaching with their colleagues." The consortium director concedes that some "continue to doubt whether educational psychology or theories of human development [have] much to tell them about teaching Racine or the topography of glacial drumlins," but he reports that all participate enthusiastically and "many...actually change their teaching."[214]

More colleges and universities should follow these leads and ensure that their faculty members and graduate students (the faculty members of tomorrow) think systematically about the pedagogy of their disciplines. This may mean finding ways to acquaint them with the literature on human learning more generally, especially as it applies to higher education—the writings of Ericson, Piaget, Kohlberg, and Gilligan, as well as Perry, Astin, Freedman, Sanford, and Chickering. It may mean reading Mary Belenky and her associates' *Women's Ways of Knowing* and Howard Gardner's *Frames of Mind*.[215] Joseph Katz and his associates, in *A New Vitality in General Education*, warn against relying too narrowly on any descriptive scheme of human development; nonetheless, they emphasize that this literature can be a good starting point for one's own thinking and close observation of the ways students learn in the specific fields one teaches.[216]

One of the few points at which the literature on the reform of undergraduate education in general has overlapped with that on the reform of teacher education is here, in a mutual recognition that college teachers need to examine more intentionally the nature of student learning in their respective fields. The authors of *Integrity in the College Curriculum* note approvingly the emergence over the last decade of this new area of research. They describe it as "indigenous" to the disciplines (and beyond the reach of pure psychology or education researchers) because it requires a "deep, expert knowledge of specific subject matter."[217] Patricia Cross is another advocate of what she terms "classroom research." She argues that teaching, properly understood, is just as intellectually demanding as research and agrees that discipline-oriented specialists are in the best position to add to both research knowledge and practical knowledge about the processes of teaching. Rather than "urging dedicated teachers to engage themselves in advanced disciplinary research," she writes, "we might better encourage them to join teaching and research in the classroom... through research on teaching and learning."[218] Cross and others also see classroom research as being most powerful when it is conducted collaboratively, with other faculty members and even with students themselves.[219]

Collaborative faculty research into pedagogy and student learning represents a promising approach to assessment—a particularly important key itself to the reform of undergraduate education. The best assurance that assessment results will be sensitive to the purposes of instruction and will be used to improve teaching is for assessment to be done, in part, by the faculty members whose courses are being evaluated. Too often, instructors have reason to see assessment as something imposed upon them with little regard for measuring the acquisition of what they really are trying to teach. If faculty members feel that the questions asked are "their questions, on issues of concern to them, answered in ways they understand and trust," they will see assessment as potentially far more useful.[220]

Joseph Katz and Mildred Henry have suggested a model that entails two faculty members working together over a semester or longer—one teaching his or her class, the other observing once a week. They interview students singly and in groups; they scrutinize exams, essays, and class notes; they reflect on the conceptual demands of the subject matter, the learning styles and progress of the students, and the relative effectiveness of different instructional strategies. These joint efforts can lead to discoveries about a course that might elude faculty members working on their own, and they can benefit both professors.[221] Whatever the collaborative model used, much can be accomplished if faculty members can be helped to rethink their reluctance to observe and evaluate one another's teaching. Making peer review of classroom teaching as common as peer review of research would, at most institutions, be a useful and worthy goal.[222]

Involving students as well as faculty members in classroom research directly serves both assessment and student learning. According to the authors of *A New Vitality in General Education*,

obtaining sustained feedback from [our students] as coinquirers into both the substance and the procedures of learning may be the single most important ingredient not only for transforming our teaching but increasing student learning. We have found again and again that when students are no longer treated as objects of our plans but are instead enlisted as coinquirers, they develop levels of reflectiveness and maturity that are surprising when we know them only from

Active inquiry, not passive absorption, is what engages students. It should pervade the curriculum

their usual behavior in the classroom and their term papers and examinations.... Their thinking will progress better if they become aware of how they think.[223]

A New Vitality describes ways to involve students in an investigation of their courses as an experience in learning, including providing them time in class for reflection on the course and on their intellectual progress in it. Other techniques can be used, but the broad strategy is powerful in that its benefits extend to so many, enforcing habits of analysis and reflection that can help keep the quality of both teaching and learning high.

Encouraging active and experiential learning

The more seriously faculty members take their teaching and the more they make it the object of their (and their colleagues' and students') study, the more they will appreciate the simple truth of Astin's observation that students learn by becoming involved.[224] Active inquiry, not passive absorption, is what engages students. It should pervade the curriculum. Frequent writing; small group discussions (especially in large classes); debates, simulations, classroom presentations, case studies, and other analytic assignments requiring a synthesizing of knowledge; clinical and community service projects; intern-

ships; independent studies; and involvement with faculty members in research—these activities, in Zelda Gamson's phrase, "change the way the faculty behave as teachers and students behave as learners."[225] None is passive; none presents learning as complete. Each creates opportunities for students to discover knowledge for themselves and requires students and teachers to place themselves in more cooperative positions.

Activity per se involves students, but analysis and careful reflection makes their experiences educative. Realizing this, some, like Ernest Lynton, have emphasized how much better we could exploit the larger world as a laboratory for undergraduate teaching—provided we are prepared to help students be thoughtful about their experiences there.[226] Experiential learning in the form of a capstone experience, senior project, or practicum is fairly common. More and more institutions, however, are establishing lower-level courses in which students examine the connection between work and liberal learning—in some cases while holding jobs and internships. Liberal arts faculty members in particular need to find more opportunities throughout the undergraduate years for students not only to achieve competence in applying their growing knowledge but to explore and reflect on its relationship to the larger world.

Strengthening academic advising

The literature on undergraduate education reform also reveals broad agreement on the need for improved "educational planning"—a phrase that conceives traditional academic advising as a more substantive and collaborative activity. The humorist Robert Benchley aptly captured the subjective side of many an undergraduate's experience in the title of his 1927 essay, "What College Did to Me." Few colleges or universities offer newly enrolled students any meaningful introduction to the purposes of higher education that would help these students wrestle with the hard questions of what they want and need from college and how best to go about getting it. Too few institutions have advising arrangements that provide more than impersonal guidance on requirements and perfunctory approval of student course schedules.[227] Students must be encouraged to take ownership of their own educational direction. They need to know—or at least be asking— how each of their academic involvements relates to the larger aims and meaning of their education, and they need to have informed and concerned help in the process.

The key is not whether faculty members or professional advisors counsel; both kinds of systems can work, just as both too often fail. The key is a commitment to advising as an institutional responsibility. Some institutions have experimented successfully with group advising of first-year students, in which one or more faculty members meet regularly with perhaps a dozen first-year students and possibly an upperclass student or two. Not only is more information shared this way; continuing informal networks of support often are formed.[228] Some colleges and universities reduce the teaching responsibilities of faculty members who are spending a significant portion of their time in academic counseling, sending a strong signal about the activity's importance.[229] The best advising systems also ensure that educational planning is a continuing and intensive process throughout students' undergraduate years.

However it is done—by professional advisors, by faculty members, by faculty-student groups, or even by 'peer advisors' working under supervision—students' educational planning must be supported with adequate materials and recognition of the professional time and effort put into it. Moreover, faculty members, administrators, and students all need to be enlightened about advising's importance as a kind of meta-education—an opportunity for collaborative reflection and planning that can bring coherence and intention to the undergraduate experience.

Promoting interdisciplinarity and curricular coherence

A particularly relevant concern of those urging the reform of undergraduate education has been overcoming the incoherence and fragmentation of the curriculum itself. The best recommendations center on creating structures so that curricular integration does not depend on exceptional personal exertions.

To promote greater connectedness among courses and programs, the top leadership of a college or university may want to consider a fundamental restructuring of the reward system. The particular *perestroika* favored by Ernest Lynton would introduce a cross-cutting flow of resources and a concomitant second channel for personnel actions. At a given institution, for example, 80 percent of available resources might continue to flow vertically, as it were, and fund the traditional research and teaching of colleges and departments—but not quite at a level sufficient to meet their needs. The remaining 20 percent would be reserved to fund interdepartmental and intercollegiate initiatives. The same faculty members would be funded for the same generic activities—teaching and research—but only to the extent that they undertake them collaboratively.[230]

Interdisciplinary teaching and research might then be a simple, universal expectation, so that a faculty member who teaches six courses a year would routinely teach one of those in cooperation with faculty members from another department. One can also imagine some of the cross-cutting flow being reserved to fund course development proposals with the most promise for creating links within the overall instructional program.

Lynton argues that many faculty members would be supportive of these changes and of the "second stream" for personnel evaluation, which would give program committees, centers, institutes, and other units involved with interdisciplinary activities more of a voice with central administrations on promotion and tenure decisions.[231] Lynton's vision is ambitious, but at many institutions where a 20 percent set-aside is impossible, 5 or 10 percent could make an important difference.

Other structural devices can encourage conversation and travel among what Michael Polanyi has termed the "overlapping neighborhoods" in which academics live—neighborhoods that Edward Said calls "disciplinary ghettos."[232] Traditional devices include joint appointments, team teaching, appointments to divisions rather than departments, and cross-listing courses. Such devices are widely used, and often they are effective. They also are sometimes used merely to create the illusion of cooperation. (Harlan Cleveland has dryly described team teaching as "that favored academic device for avoiding interdisciplinary thought.")[233]

Less traditional is Gerald Graff's suggestion of structured "teacher-swapping," the opening of one's classroom to colleagues who take differing and even conflicting approaches.[234] This proposal has the merit of de-emphasizing any too-facile identification of "common ground" and letting students experience the differences among disciplines and approaches *as differences*; in Graff's phrase, it "reconceive[s] educational coherence as a coherence of conflict rather than of consensus"—which is, in some environments, perhaps the best that can be hoped for.[235]

Between these two extremes of tactics familiar and new are other imaginative and proven ones not yet widely used. Many campuses now have curricular task forces to revitalize their general-education programs. Some of these are merely tinkering with requirements; others are bringing faculty members together for reasoned, collaborative consideration of how better integrated and less redundant coverage of key materials and modes of enquiry might be achieved.[236] Institutions should convene similar task forces to look at upper-level as well as lower-level coursework, especially in cognate disciplines. The challenge has been described by Carol Schneider as one of connecting assignments "within courses, across courses, and across years of college."[237] This is an enormous task, even when there is agreement that it should be done. To be effective, task forces need the resources to free faculty members for this work and reward those who do it. Funds must be available for the collaborative efforts that produce new courses and for the professional development that will enable faculty members to teach them well.

In addition to coordinating current courses and redesigning them along more integrative lines, colleges and universities might consider adding certain offerings specifically to provide connective tissue. In the "federated learning communities" pioneered at the State University of New York–Stony Brook, groups of students enroll together in a series of six courses—three per semester—that relate to some broad theme such as world hunger. The faculty members for these courses bring their distinctive approaches to the subject in a jointly conducted core seminar, and a seventh—a "master learner" who joins the students in all these courses—leads a linking seminar that attempts an integration. The model is elaborate, but institutions could enjoy many of its benefits simply by creating some "linking seminars" of their own. Introducing little indepen-

There are a number of administrative structures and strategies that can ensure attention to and support for the work that must be done

dent content but helping students explore in a focused way the interrelation of two or more subjects, these seminars can be an effective—and, for participating faculty members, rewarding—means of fostering new coherence in undergraduate education.[238]

The ideas reviewed in this section derive from a body of writing that makes little specific reference to the education of teachers. They have important implications, however, for improving colleges and universities as settings in which teachers are prepared. They describe academic environments that would foster in large numbers of students the qualities and habits of mind that might dispose them to teach, and that—even without programs specifically for future teachers—would begin to equip them for that job.

Undergraduates who see their arts and sciences professors take teaching seriously and study teaching and learning in the disciplines; who experience learning as both an active and reflective process; who, through good advising and integrative academic coursework, discover overarching purposes and larger structures of understanding—these undergraduates would be ideal material from which to fashion teachers for the schools. Drawing on their "apprenticeships," they would transform rather than enforce the status quo.

ADMINISTRATIVE STRUCTURES AND STRATEGIES

Institutional leaders can take many steps more directly aimed at improving the education of prospective teachers. First, there are a number of administrative structures and strategies that can ensure attention to and support for the work that must be done.

A campus-wide committee on the education of teachers can be essential in making the entire college or university a setting for teacher preparation. Such "all-campus" committees are common, but they are often dormant; when active, their chief concern often is with symbolic accommodations intended to leave the programs they represent essentially undisturbed.[239] However, when properly constituted and given a clear mandate, strong support, and appropriate leadership these committees can be effective.

A committee on the education of teachers, for example, should represent the faculty and administration of all key areas within education and the arts and sciences. Liberal arts faculty members on the committee should be individuals who are respected by their peers as scholars and teachers and whose word carries weight in departmental councils. The chairs of key departments should be active members. The committee as a whole may best be chaired by the dean of arts and sciences or of education, or co-chaired by both.

An appropriate first charge for such a committee would be a comprehensive institutional audit. This self-study should reach well beyond the academic program. Does the institution send applicants unintended messages that discourage their considering careers in teaching? What impact do the institution's financial aid programs have on those considering the field? Are the needs of future teachers met by the current system of academic advising and by the institution's career counseling and placement service? Does the institution recognize—perhaps with special awards or profiles in alumni magazines—the contributions of its own alumni who are school teachers or outstanding teachers from the local schools?

An all-campus committee also should take the lead in educating faculty members to the deep common interests they share with teachers in the schools, to the conditions that prevail there, and, ultimately, to the ways in which colleges and faculty members can become involved. It can encourage faculty members to visit schools, host campus visits by school professionals, and work to have well-qualified practictioners appointed as adjunct or visiting faculty members. It can identify faculty members' interests and broker a variety of productive arrangements, alerting faculty members to opportunities to serve as consultants in specific curricular areas or to entire systems, for example, or to take the schools as a major subject of their research. Through such involvements psychologists, historians, anthropologists, economists, sociologists, and linguists, among others, can employ the tools of their disciplines in especially useful ways.[240]

The core work of such a committee, however, is breaking down disciplinary boundaries within the curriculum. It needs to look for overlap and potential linkages among courses and work with curriculum committees to improve cross-departmental coordination. It needs to see that all academic advisors understand the requirements facing those who seek certification. It needs to be able to recommend released time and leave support for faculty members to redesign courses. It needs to help departments find a calculus by which faculty members who team teach or teach in another discipline can be credited appropriately for their effort. It needs to identify opportunities for hiring on the divisional rather than the departmental level and for making joint appointments between education and other departments. It must ensure that both the economic and the professional status of faculty members willing to undertake new involvements is protected—a requirement implying a voice both in the allocation of resources and in decisions on promotion and tenure.

In light of this last point and the level of activity this committee would need to sustain, some institutions might want to establish it as an advisory group to an appropriate senior administrator who would have the authority, funding, and staff to carry out its recommendations. Linda Bunnell-Jones has argued that "the wisest approach to campus-wide responsibility for teacher education [may be] a new, broader concept of the role of dean or director of the school of education. He or she should not only preside over the professional education faculty but should also be responsible for integrating the arts and sciences faculty and the teacher education faculty."[241] So long as the dean or director were given powers to match his or her expanded responsibility, this assignment—and the empowerment of the committee as an advisory body—would make sense in many settings. In a way appropriate to the cross-disciplinary character of teacher preparation, these steps would give the dean or director cross-disciplinary responsibility—an approach now used successfully in numerous institutions with deans of under-

graduate or graduate studies. They also would strengthen the dean's or director's hand by ensuring the formal involvement and backing of the academic leaders most critical to his or her success.

Most colleges and universities do not need to create *ex nihilo* a process by which a liberal arts major can complete requirements for certification. Most already have one—however humble or obscured by the typically much larger enterprise of traditional teacher education. In order to find out about these arrangements—which we refer to as "certification programs," although often they are less structured than the term implies— AAC in 1987 conducted a nationwide survey. The data provide for the first time a basic descriptive profile of these programs—their numbers, locations, enrollments, administrative structures, requirements, and the like. Analysis also suggests the kinds of traits that characterize the most viable of them. The survey results are reported in Chapter Nine. A few, however, are relevant to our present discussion of administrative strategies. They have something to teach us about what works and what does not in these programs, on which many institutions will need to build in their efforts to do more.

The all-college or all-university committee can benefit any campus that prepares teachers, whether through conventional teacher education majors, certification programs for arts and sciences majors, or both. One lesson from AAC's survey, however, is that certification programs for arts and sciences majors also are well-served when they have their own oversight and governance group. The survey found that the more viable programs were those most conscious of themselves as entities. They were more likely to operate formally and to be well-known and widely supported on their campuses. An active, broadly representative oversight, advisory, or governing committee—which the programs in the top tier of the survey tend to have—apparently can do much to give a program the kind of identity, visibility, and broad involvement it needs to thrive. To prevent committees from proliferating unnecessarily, the certification program's oversight group might be constituted as a subcommittee of the all-campus body. In any event, the two committees' functions would be similar, they would need to involve many of the same parties, and their work would need to be closely coordinated.

The survey results suggest that active management is critical. The more viable certification programs secure cooperation from faculty members in different disciplines, develop formal procedures for recruit-

ing, keep careful student records, and make special scheduling efforts. Indeed, it appears to be more important that the program be actively managed than that any particular figure on campus direct it—for example, the head of education or someone from the arts and sciences. One variable that seems to have no bearing on the viability of a certification program is the way in which an institution structures teacher education—that is, as a school, college, department, or program. A program that is relatively formal and actively managed and that secures support from all parts of the campus can prosper within any kind of administrative arrangement.

Finally, the survey results suggest some of the different ways liberal arts faculty members can be encouraged to become involved in certification programs. The most common role is serving on a program oversight committee. Other key roles include team teaching with education faculty members, serving as academic advisors to certification students, working with or supervising student teachers, and participating in program administration. Institutional leaders and those with direct oversight over certification programs need to find the incentives that will motivate arts and sciences faculty members to involve themselves in these ways. They can think about

The general education of prospective teachers must be extensive and rigorous enough to appeal to strong students

these roles as being on a continuum that moves from relatively passive to extraordinarily active involvements—and along which faculty members can be encouraged to progress as they develop understanding, skill, and commitment.[242]

The work to be done lends itself to step-by-step efforts in other ways, too. Integration can be achieved with one department at a time. The shrewdest course for developing a modest certification program into a larger, well-integrated one may be to focus on establishing links with one or two key departments—for example, English and mathematics. Success in a test case or two can establish the certification program's potential and interest other arts and sciences departments in its possibilities.

We turn now from issues of administrative structure and strategy to recommendations having to do more directly with the course of study of arts and sciences majors preparing for careers in teaching. We group these in three broad categories: general education and liberal arts electives, study in the major, and study in professional education.

GENERAL EDUCATION AND LIBERAL ARTS ELECTIVES

In recent years, most U.S. institutions have claimed to be rethinking their general education requirements.[243] Yet in 1988 it was still possible to graduate from nearly 80 percent of four-year institutions without a course in a foreign language. Sixty-two percent had no requirement in philosophy, 45 percent had no requirement in American or English literature, and 37 percent had no requirement for any course in history. We lack comparable national figures on science and mathematics requirements, but recent transcript studies indicate that few colleges and universities provide students with substantial introductions to those areas.[244]

Although decisions about the content of general education are an institutional prerogative, and arguments for a universal "canon" properly have been resisted, many colleges and universities should give more thought to whether their curricula expose students to essential subject matter and approaches—in ways, moreover, that serve the aims of general education. The typical American university provides a loose framework of distribution requirements, an array of hundreds or even thousands of more or less narrowly conceived courses that are said to meet them, and little guidance to students choosing among options.[245] Solving these problems entails tightening general-education requirements, reducing the number of courses approved as meeting them, ensuring that those remaining are broadly conceived and not merely introductions to the respective academic majors, and giving students more help in choosing appropriately among these offerings.

The general education of prospective teachers, in particular, must be extensive and rigorous enough to appeal to strong students and support a career that draws widely and sometimes deeply on essential fields of knowledge. Whether general education is presented in conventional disciplinary form or not, it should include substantial work with the subject matter and approaches of each of the major curricular domains: the humanities, social sciences, natural sciences, mathematics, and fine arts. It should include no courses designed to present these students with general-education subject matter in simplified form (for example, a special general-education section of mathematics for elementary school teachers). It should develop all the skills, understandings, and habits of mind that are essential to any undergraduate and emphasize an integrated understanding of the different subjects it encompasses.

The general-education component provides colleges and universities some of their best opportunities for recruiting liberal arts majors to teaching. Perhaps because we have accepted an erroneous equation of education with pedagogy, only a minority of institutions—36 percent, according to AAC survey data reported in Chapter Nine—now offer any education-related courses for general-education credit. Yet education is arguably the only discipline whose main concern is with teaching and learning. An education or "educational studies" course that approaches these subjects broadly would be an entirely appropriate part of most general-education programs. Most students become parents concerned with the education of children; all become payers of school taxes, and most vote on educational issues or elect candidates who do.[246]

Like improved advising and opportunities for classroom research, an educational studies course might help students reflect on the intellectual purposes and experiences of their own college careers. George Kneller has argued forcefully for the place of such a course in the general-education curriculum.

> The subject matter—for quality of content and intellectual rigor [matching] any syllabus in the undergraduate curriculum...[would not be] limited to, or even geared toward, the preparation of teachers any more than courses in sociology are intended to prepare social workers, or courses in English to

prepare writers and journalists. [Its purpose would be] to provide knowledge and understanding of education and to challenge students of all specialties to think more deeply and more imaginatively about education....[247]

More importantly still, broadly conceived courses in educational studies might bring some good students into teaching.[248] Such courses can interest arts and sciences students in educational issues early in their academic careers when they realistically consider a course of study leading to certification. Now, in most settings, education does not participate in the competition for student interest that general education in part represents.

General education also can interest arts and sciences students in teaching if it contains a component of service. Most service rendered by college students is now done on a volunteer, noncredit basis. Increasing numbers of institutions, however, are finding that when properly designed and integrated—for example, as part of a broad course on philanthropy, volunteerism, and public service— "service learning" is creditworthy. There is little question about its benefits. One study found, for example, that 90 percent of student volunteers considered their service at least as valuable to them as classroom work. Tutoring, a typical service activity,

has been found significantly to increase students' altruism, empathy, self-esteem, and academic average.[249]

Service learning can sustain undergraduates' idealism and foster in them a disposition to serve others— sometimes through teaching.[250] This point is borne out by a recent evaluation of the Educational Commission of the States' Partners in Learning Project. The project links volunteer college student mentors with elementary and secondary students (in grades 4–9) who are at risk eventually of dropping out. In addition to the effort's anticipated benefits, surprising numbers of the college students who had participated expressed a new interest in pursuing careers as teachers in the schools.[251]

A well-planned program of general and elective liberal arts education can help liberal arts majors complete their certification requirements within four years. Curricular integration and informed advising should enable students to use general-education courses and liberal arts electives to meet all prerequisites and at least some professional education requirements.

Although situations differ from state to state, there is a tendency on the part of those who design education curricula to translate state requirements for coverage of particular subjects and competencies into separate professional courses or parts thereof. The program descriptions in Chapter Ten, however, demonstrate that institutions can succeed in showing state agencies how prospective teachers can acquire necessary skills and knowledge through general education and other liberal arts curricula already in place. By looking to general education and liberal arts courses for "professional" content, they have managed both to hold down the unnecessary proliferation of professional courses and better to integrate the study of education into the liberal arts.

Institutional program planners and state agencies alike need to have a more flexible conception, then, of where in the curriculum—including the general-education curriculum—relevant material might be found. They also should bear in mind that while some materials will always be the province of specialized curricula, premature specialization discourages students of broad interests, and it reduces the amount of intellectual experience they have with students from other academic and professional areas.[252] More importantly still, by providing professional education content through courses that are technically focused, we sometimes forgo opportunities to deal with the content in its full context and intellectual richness.

We may need, as Edward J. Meade

has argued, to put more emphasis on understanding child and adolescent development through the broader social sciences perspectives of anthropology and sociology—not just that of pyschology, which he describes as "too dominant and...too limited."[253] The study of political science and economics can deepen insight into contemporary social conditions relevant to the schools. Knowledge that teachers need can also be found in the humanities. Writers, philosophers, and historians provide memorable descriptions of what it has been to teach and be taught in different times and places and timeless enquiries into the nature and purposes of education. The truth and power of their representations can enrich any prospective teacher's training.[254]

STUDY IN THE MAJOR

Students majoring in arts and sciences fields and preparing to teach should complete academic majors fully as rigorous and demanding as those of other students in their fields. It is not clear, however, that most majors, as they are now conceived, serve either group of students well—or that the two groups' courses of study should be the same.

Despite assertions that more extensive academic majors will cure what ails teachers, effective reform de-

Effective reform depends...
on redesigning the major in ways that will serve all students

pends at least as much on redesigning study-in-depth in ways that will serve all students. We have suggested the kinds of changes that are needed. They would put less emphasis on the knowledge a discipline has produced and more on the methods and styles of enquiry it employs. They would encourage new attention to a field's assumptions, its scope and its limitations, its ways of organizing and integrating knowledge, its relations to other disciplines, and its applications in and implications for the world at large. Such redesign of the academic major would represent a significant change in American higher education, helping to displace progressively specialized preparation for advanced, graduate-level study as the major's organizing paradigm. Many would argue that it would increase the major's value not only to those who, like prospective school teachers, are pursuing other commitments but to future disciplinary specialists themselves.

In addition to reorienting study-in-depth for all students, we should recognize that future teachers may need to choose some courses that are different from those their fellow majors take. Some argue that to allow this—or anything less than a full four years of study in the arts and sciences—is to compromise subject mastery.[255] There is no defense to be made for watered-down courses or truncated programs. We do need to be more thoughtful, however, about equating length with quality and recognize that certain courses are more essential than others to those who will teach in the schools. Our concern should be that students aspiring to teach complete a major as rigorous as any, providing professional levels of subject mastery; it should not be to enroll them in a program indistinguishable from their peers'.

The prospective teacher's academic major thus may need to include courses not among those taken most often by fellow students in the department—advanced composition and linguistics for the English major, for example, or courses offering advanced work in algebra, trigonometry, and geometry for the student majoring in math.[256] Faculty members can help prospective teachers by adding appropriate new dimensions to their courses and by providing students with opportunities to explore on their own topics of special relevence to their chosen work. These might include, for example, opportunities to do a research paper, within a course on the Victorian novel, on the children's literature of that period, or a field study in urban sociology that focuses on some aspect of the local schools.

The academic major also can contribute to prospective teachers' education by ensuring their reflection on how the material within the field might be taught most effectively. In one local version of what we have earlier termed "classroom research," Stanford University education majors are encouraged to become students of the teaching they receive in the arts and sciences. They observe and describe (sometimes in case study formats) instances of teaching that bear analysis and annotation, using their liberal arts professors both as subjects and resources, talking with them about aims and strategies.[257] Liberal arts majors aspiring to teach can do this as well, and arts and sciences professors should support them in their efforts. There is no better place than an advanced course within his or her discipline for a liberal arts professor to confront the misperception that formal study of teaching and learning are reserved for educationists.[258]

A related strategy ensures attention to subject-specific pedagogy within the major by offering adjunct experiences with key courses in the discipline. Most arts and sciences majors include a core of courses that present, more than others, material that is taught in the schools. For a college English major, for example, the surveys of English and American literature and courses in Shakespeare, modern poetry, the American novel, and minority and women's literature would account for much of

the literature taught in the secondary curriculum. Teacher education and liberal arts faculty members together might provide students enrolled in such central courses with regular opportunities to discuss the pedagogical demands and possibilities of the material they are studying.[259] These discussions also might involve practicing teachers and curriculum designers from the schools.

These adjunct experiences could be voluntary, noncredit preceptorials or, preferably, mini-courses carrying one unit of credit. In the latter case, a series of six such courses would be the equivalent of two full three-hour courses and would reduce the total time available for traditional work in the major and in education by one course each. This loss would be more than offset, however, by the deepening of the participating students' understanding both of the material and of how it can be taught. An additional and very desirable benefit would be a diminished need for separate special methods courses.

Another essential support for students majoring in the liberal arts and preparing to teach is informed advising, preferably provided by two faculty members—one from education and the other in the student's major department. The programs of these students permit them little margin for error in course selection, yet not all departmental advisors know certification requirements and the particular courses that might serve prospective teachers best. It is critical, therefore, that liberal arts departments have one or more advisors designated, willing, and able to assist these students. The greater the stature of the faculty members assuming this role, moreover, the likelier it is that the concerns of prospective teachers will be taken seriously around the campus.

Departmentally based advisors can help arts and sciences majors who plan to teach overcome the frequent loneliness of their efforts to negotiate the requirements of two curricula. This loneliness often stems from the student's not knowing or having contact with other students who are doing the same thing. Effective socialization to a profession often results from the sense of being part of a group—a cohort that finds its identity precisely in overcoming some kind of collective trial.[260] The faculty advisor who brings prospective teachers together—perhaps even with their peers from other departments—reinforces these students' commitment at a time and in ways critical to their perseverance and success.

More needs to be said, finally, about the suitability of a liberal arts major for those intending to teach at the elementary level. Some have called for all prospective teachers to complete a liberal arts major. We urge that all secondary teachers do so. There is a legitimate question, however, regarding teachers in the lower grades. Ernest Boyer has reminded us that the basic test of a major is whether it has "legitimate intellectual content...and...the capacity to enlarge rather than narrow the vision of the student.[261] Since a well-conceived major in elementary education theoretically can meet both tests and still allow adequate work and sometimes even a second major or minor in the arts and sciences, the judgment should be a local one, based on an assessment of the strengths of the people and programs currently in place in both curricular areas.

We must bear in mind that elementary teachers teach as generalists, not specialists, in the self-contained classroom. Moreover, it has been "urged on both psychological and social grounds that elementary schools tend to be far more effective than the secondary schools precisely because they treat the child as a whole person" and knowledge is presented in a coherent way.[262] Thus, one cannot be sanguine about the single discipline major as appropriate preparation, at least as it is usually now conceived.

That said, however, we stress that an undergraduate elementary education major should not be required of elementary teachers any more than a business degree is required of those going into business. Indeed, we strongly endorse for prospective elementary teachers the benefits of liberal arts majors conceived along broader lines. Specifically, the combination of a substantial general education and an interdisciplinary liberal arts major could give elementary teachers a much stronger grounding in all content areas of the elementary school and depth in at least two of these areas.

The latter goal is important. As the Carnegie report points out, an elementary teacher's wider span of responsibility cannot excuse a less-than-rigorous grasp of subjects.[263] Teachers who have delved and obtained a degree of mastery are more able to mediate their subjects in a variety of ways, better equipped to continue learning on their own, and readier for professional autonomy. These are *desiderata* for all teachers, regardless of grade level. Students expecting to teach older elementary children—those in grades four through six, where some division of instruction among several teachers is increasingly common—might consider either an interdisciplinary or a disciplinary liberal arts major. The key would be that it permit the requisite breadth, depth, and integration of study.

STUDY IN PROFESSIONAL EDUCATION

For the last half century, the essential professional education component—referred to above as the "certification program" for liberal arts majors—has remained essentially unchanged.[264] It varies in detail from state to state and among institutions, but almost everywhere it consists broadly of work in "foundations" and "methods" and supervised experience in practice teaching.

Virtually everyone outside teacher education who has an opinion on the matter believes that what most needs to be done to improve this curriculum is to make it more rigorous, more substantive, and less trivial. Teacher educators understandably resent being tarred indiscriminately with this broad brushstroke. Many certification programs are in fact quite strong. Indeed, there is evidence—potentially discomfiting for some in the arts and sciences—that students taking the widely derided methods courses generally find these at least as demanding as their regular courses in English and history (though less so than their courses in science and math).[265]

Even teacher educators, however, acknowledge that their discipline has let its standards remain too low for too long. Although, in fairness, the reasons often have had less to do

The failure of teacher educators to offer challenging, well-regarded courses has deprived them of strong students

with teacher educators themselves than with the agendas of others, the effects have been costly. The frequent awarding of credit for work that is "reasonable as a prerequisite for teaching but inappropriate for upper-level study" has often prevented education programs from gaining the respect and support of faculty members and senior administrators in other fields.[266] The failure of teacher educators to offer challenging, well-regarded courses has deprived them of strong students. The students they have attracted, moreover, often believe they gain little from their studies. According to one disturbing 1987 report, fewer than half of the education students surveyed felt that their program contributed to their development of "academic, scholarly and intellectual qualities," and only 57 percent felt it helped them develop skills in critical thinking.[267]

Strengthening the professional education component requires both better integration of its internal parts and better integration externally with the arts and sciences. As Alan Tom has observed, in teacher education, as in the arts and sciences, programs generally are structured in a way that allows discrete courses to be taught by specialists—in methods, for example, or educational psychology.[268] In education, as in the arts and sciences, this practice produces

fragmentation. While some courses overlap unnecessarily, others fail to touch and reinforce each other as they should. Foundations courses are roundly dismissed as being too theoretical, methods courses as being sterile and technical, and practice teaching as being insufficiently educative. Ending the segregation of theory, methods, and practice and seeing that these elements enrich one another is essential.

Equally important, however, are efforts to unite the arts and sciences and education and emphasize the latter field's several strong disciplinary bases.[269] External integration can increase the professional education component's rigor and substance and give arts and sciences faculty members a sense of investment in the component; it also can provide excellent opportunities for consolidating required education coursework in ways that facilitate graduation within four years.

Foundations

Courses in the "foundations" of education—social, psychological, philosophical, historical, legal, economic, and the like—provide students the theoretical underpinnings for further professional study. They "[examine] the dynamics of context forces, [and question] assumptions; [they explore] ethical implications... and...the fundamental questions which relate to the heart of [education's] purposes."[270] Introduced into the professional education program "to assure that theory would be considered in the training of teachers," foundations courses present the intellectual bases for methods of teaching. They help ensure that students will not teach mechanically and be unable, as some teachers are, to improve on methods that have become dysfunctional.[271] For these and other reasons, foundations courses are important to the maintenance and enrichment of liberal learning within the education curriculum.

It is ironic, then, that one consequence of the school and teacher-education reform movement has been to reduce the time devoted to foundations. In their haste to mandate pragmatic changes, many state agencies have increased the time students are required to spend in practice teaching; in their assumed need to delete something, many colleges and universities reluctantly have reduced their requirements in foundations.[272] These changes have not displeased the critics of foundations courses. Students, teachers, and teacher educators variously dismiss them as irrelevant and too theoretical; urge that they be postponed to the in-service level, where they might mean more to teachers with two to three years of experience;[273] and charge that they reflect no

agreement from institution to institution on proper content and compress various snatches of material into offerings that do little to help the student see education as a whole.[274]

Several steps can help correct the deficiences of foundations courses and realize their potential.[275] Ideally, foundations courses should be jointly planned and jointly taught by faculty members from education and the liberal arts. They might be more effective if they eschewed "problems-" or "topics-" or "issues-in-education" approaches, providing instead a comprehensive framework for all subsequent professional coursework. Drawing deeply on education's disciplinary bases, they then could cover more coherently the history of American education and key philosophies of education and the schools, and they could make more use of economics, political science, anthropology, and other arts and sciences. Multicultural concerns are addressed increasingly now, but foundations courses might usefully offer a comparative perspective on educational systems as well.

In addition to strengthening the content, scope, and coherence of foundations courses, those who teach them should find ways to incorporate active modes of learning. They also need to clarify more aggressively how an understanding of the material covered supports good teaching and effective schools. Experiential learning components may help in both these connections. Relatively few foundations courses now involve any form of clinical work or field observation and research. Yet the possibilities for out-of-classroom investigation are, if anything, more numerous here than in traditional arts and sciences courses.

In the area of psychological foundations, for example, courses in human development generally will be preferable to narrower translations of psychology for teachers, especially ones that neglect the whole human lifespan to focus exclusively on the early period of childhood to late adolescence. Now often taught either by psychology, education, or even human ecology (home economics) departments, according to the vagaries of local circumstance, human development courses can be interdisciplinary and team-taught. In addition to incorporating relevent perspectives from education and psychology, they can be strengthened by the cross-cultural and ethnographic sophistication of sociology and anthropology. The human development course can be an important point at which to infuse research findings and research skills, and it presents exceptional opportunities for helping students become active enquirers. Every such course can include clinical experiences in

which prospective teachers pursue investigations that include gathering and analyzing data, observing school children, interviewing different age groups, and assessing themselves as learners. Such a course can be conceived broadly enough to merit general-education credit and, with its rich integration of theory and clinical work, a key experience in both liberal and professional education.

Methods

Coursework in the theory and practice of curriculum development and instructional methods—widely known as "methods"—generally falls into two areas: "general" or generic methods and "special" or subject-specific methods. According to AAC survey data, prospective teachers generally take one course in the former. Students preparing for careers in the secondary schools usually take, in addition, one course in the latter—in that content area of the secondary curriculum in which they plan to teach—plus one in the "teaching of reading" in that content area. Prospective elementary school teachers typically take one methods course in each of the four principal subject areas of the elementary school curriculum—science, mathematics, language arts, and social studies— plus one in the teaching of reading.

Teaching is an activity that lends itself to strategies, styles, and techniques.[276] Instruction in methods, therefore, can serve a very useful purpose. There is no question that teachers need to know the "texts, workbooks, exercises, experiments... that are appropriate for teaching various age groups."[277] Thoughtful people within and outside the field, however, question whether the methods courses typically offered do not do as much harm as good. They claim so much time—according to several studies, an average of more than nineteen hours in the case of prospective elementary school teachers—that they can prevent a student from obtaining within four years both a liberal arts degree and teacher certification.[278] In addition, more than any other part of the professional curriculum, methods courses have a reputation for triviality that repels strong students and potential collaborators on arts and sciences faculties. For these reasons, institutions should rethink their traditional assumptions about the ways methods instruction needs to be packaged and the kinds of activities of which it consists.

Consolidation of methods instruction is a desirable and achievable goal. Some in education argue flatly that there is "little transferability from one area of the curriculum to another...[that, for example,] the methods and materials necessary to teach reading effectively have little

relation to [those used for] science."[279] Others, however, acknowledge considerable redundancy—with special methods courses needlessly repeating coverage of planning and curriculum and emphasizing the same broad kinds of strategies. They argue that much would be gained by combining the now-separate methods courses.[280] In addition to obvious economies, consolidation would create new opportunities for displaying commonalities and differences among approaches to the several content areas.

One model might be a content-rich, carefully integrated, five-hour course combining all study of general and special methods. Taken for one semester by prospective secondary teachers and for two by those preparing for the elementary schools, this course could handle general topics (including some now treated in special methods courses) in common sessions, with preceptorials for each of the content areas. Clinical "laboratory" sessions could supplement both common and special work, and faculty members could enforce throughout a new attention to theory—the critical framework in which methods need to be understood.

A key purpose of studying methods is acquiring "pedagogical content knowledge"—Lee Shulman's term, again, for the subject- and learner-specific knowledge one needs in order to teach. Thus, arts and sciences faculty members should be involved in teaching conventional methods courses. We also have suggested that departments provide prospective teachers with adjunct courses in association with certain core departmental offerings and that in these courses liberal arts faculty members join teacher educators (and possibly experienced, graduate-degreed practitioners from the schools) in exploring the pedagogical demands and possibilities of particular material. Such discipline-based courses would provide ideal settings for special methods instruction.

A critical ingredient for any methods course, wherever it is based, is this combination of faculty perspective and expertise. General methods typically are taught by education faculty members. Special methods, however—which must be taught by someone who is certified—may be taught by someone in the arts and sciences who is certified, by an education faculty member with some academic background in the relevant content area, or by a teacher from the schools. Clearly, each solution has attendant risks and shortcomings as a way of imparting a high level of pedagogical content knowledge. A strong course in methods requires an extraordinary collaboration that builds on the strengths of mainstream liberal arts faculty mem-

bers, teacher educators, and practicing teachers, allowing them to complement each other and compensate for one another's deficiencies.

In addition to making methods instruction more efficient, the kinds of changes recommended here should help reverse the intellectual impoverishment that results from methods' separation from the liberal arts. They will enrich methods courses, moreover, not only with the content but with the approaches of those fields as well. A recent publication from the Consortium for Excellence in Teacher Education, a group of teacher education programs in east coast institutions, describes this latter benefit:

Even in those education courses which are primarily grounded in practice, namely practice teaching and curriculum and methods, the liberal arts...[have] a powerful influence.... Each aspect of the teaching process is examined systematically using the inquiry approaches that characterize other areas of the students' liberal education. Hypothesis testing, problem-solving and decision making—all critical for effective practice—are combined with research findings, experiential data and intuition to develop individuals who engage in teaching both as an art and as a science.[281]

In short, as these changes bring together liberal arts and teacher education faculty members and in-service teachers—and as all of these begin to challenge and extend one another and their students in a common examination of how to teach—fewer students will be able to think that the question is ever simply, "what method?" They will learn to grapple with the formulation, "What method, for what purpose, with what material, with what students, in what circumstances?" and they will learn to ask this question of themselves and of their schools.[282]

Practice teaching

Socrates suggested that the young be led to the edge of the battlefield; teacher educators send their charges into the schools.[283] The nature and extent of practice teaching varies greatly. According to a recent AACTE study, however, practice teachers spend an average of thirty hours a week in a classroom for a full twelve-week semester. During this time they work principally under the supervision of one cooperating teacher. A college or university supervisor—usually a member of the education faculty—visits an average of six or seven times during the semester (for an hour each time, on average) to observe the student's teaching, examine his or her materials and lesson plans, talk with the cooperating teacher, and evaluate the student's progress. The student generally teaches by himself or herself for two or three weeks during the period and assumes the full load of the cooperating teacher. Colleges and universities award an average of ten semester hours for practice teaching and often require a related seminar so that a full credit load is carried for the semester.[284]

Believing that experience is the best teacher, many states in recent years have mandated more extensive practice teaching. Teachers do tend to rate their own practice teaching experiences highly, sometimes looking back on them as one of the few parts of their college programs that subsequently had any direct usefulness to them in their classrooms.[285] Nonetheless, many teacher educators have deep reservations about practice teaching. They recognize that it is essential but think that too often it fails to serve the purposes it should.

Practice teaching falls short on several counts. Like the study of theory in foundations courses and techniques in methods courses, too often it is segregated from the rest of what should be an internally integrated professional curriculum. Supervisors may not be well informed about the preceding professional curriculum; cooperating teachers, who are rarely trained for their role as mentors, tend to be even less well informed.[286]

Practice teaching does not need to be lengthened; it needs to be made more educative

Student teachers often are not given enough field experience prior to practice teaching to learn from their experience. The seminars that accompany student teaching have been said to "concentrate on mastery of technique and management, rather than encouraging careful examination of experience."[287] Even insofar as technique is concerned, research shows that field experience often leads to a narrowing rather than an expanding of students' repertoires, as they discontinue skills learned in the program and adopt those of the cooperating teacher.[288]

Practice teaching does not need to be lengthened; it needs to be made more educative. We need, first, to be more careful about its supervision. Colleges and universities use a wide variety of professionals to supervise student teaching, from regular education faculty members, to part-time and adjunct faculty members (who may be specially trained teachers from the schools), to graduate students. Whoever assumes the role—and there is disagreement about who is most appropriate—must be thoroughly trained. He or she should help the student connect academic content with experience and reflect on their interrelationship both in an accompanying seminar and during conferences in the school. Supervisors tend to carry heavy loads, inconsistent with giving high-quality

attention to their charges. It would be a wise use of their resources for many colleges and universities to reduce the number of students assigned to each supervisor; supervisors then could give the extensive "feedback and follow-up coaching" that research suggests students need if practice teaching is to have any value.[289]

Practice teaching should provoke consideration of content and how it is taught in addition to general pedagogy. Thus, arts and sciences faculty members have a critical role to play. An effective arrangement can team an education professor, who serves as overall supervisor, with a liberal arts faculty member who also visits the school site (sometimes with his or her colleague and sometimes alone) to work with the student teacher specifically on the teaching of particular material. Institutions lacking the resources to hire additional supervisors within education may see in the increased involvement of liberal arts faculty members both an economically feasible and educationally desirable way of supplementing the efforts of the current staff.

The value of field experience depends, as Judith Lanier has pointed out, "on prospective teachers' being properly prepared to learn from it."[290] Students need to be engaged from the outset of their professional study in a developmental sequence of guided practica that teaches them to join field experience with reflection. The curriculum should systematically integrate field work and other forms of experiential learning into the study of both foundations and methods. The sequence of practica itself should represent "a clear progression in the level of expectation and the complexity of the teaching required"—moving, for example, from observation, through "microteaching" in a structured situation, to teaching an entire class.[291] The sequence of practica should begin early, so that students unsuited to careers in the schools can be directed to other programs. The time it requires—indeed, the time students need to develop into beginning teachers—is itself an argument against crowding teacher education into a relatively brief graduate-level program.

Finally, even if student teachers know first-hand the kind of "thoughtful trial and error" required to learn from experience, and even if the structure of the practice teaching experience and the faculty members who guide it both enforce reflection and constant reference to larger concerns, practice teaching can fail if coordinating teachers are not properly prepared.[292] Ninety-eight percent of the student teacher's time is supervised by these individuals, and they exercise enormous influence.[293] Ken-

neth Howey is entirely correct in insisting that "institutions of higher education...join hands with teacher organizations to lobby for monies to support the training and selection of master teachers" who might take mentoring as a primary function.[294]

Induction and in-service training
Teacher educators use the terms "induction" to refer to the introduction of new graduates into the teaching profession and "in-service training" to refer to the continuing education they receive. These postbaccalaureate experiences are themselves a critical part of the liberal education of teachers.

Although new teachers are as much learners as they are teachers and are not yet capable of handling many of the challenges the classroom presents, few states or school districts provide them significant, organized programs of support.[295] Twenty states have no formal state-sponsored programs at all to induct new teachers, and meaningful mentoring relationships are said to be the exception rather than the rule. As a result, too many new teachers experience an abrupt and unstaged introduction to practice; they assume the full duties of the classroom teacher from their first day.[296] This sink-or-swim situation often leads new teachers to focus on controlling student behavior rather than on fostering learning. They develop coping strategies and approaches that simply repeat those of earlier generations.[297]

The experiences of the first year or two of teaching need to be mediated, even if only indirectly, by teacher educators. Yet most education programs have lost contact with those they recommend for certification by the time these graduates enter the school classroom.[298] There is little they can do about this, given the many schools—often distant—in which new graduates take positions. Yet every collegiate program should accept some involvement in a systematic program of induction for local teachers as a basic professional function.[299] Many may find their most appropriate role to be training teachers selected to serve as mentors.

Among the most promising induction models to have emerged in recent years are those in which school administrators and teachers' unions "alter existing arrangements for assigning resources, students, and classrooms so that beginning teachers no longer get what no one else wants."[300] Traditionally, teachers with seniority are given preference for "desirable" assignments; new teachers take the places they vacate, often in more depressed schools, where they have disproportionately fewer opportunities to learn from talented and experienced peers.[301] Some districts, however, have turned the system around, des-

ignating schools with high turnover as "induction schools," which they then provide with additional resources and staff with a careful mix of experienced and novice teachers.[302] Some districts, like Charlotte-Mecklenburg, North Carolina, and Rochester, New York, have introduced a career ladder with the explicit expectation that those designated as master teachers would have a special responsibility for mentoring in such schools.[303] This kind of arrangement meets multiple needs at once. Teachers are recognized for their talent and experience, new teachers are assisted by seasoned peers, and those students most at risk get more of the kind of help they need.

These innovations suggest the "development schools" and "clinical schools" envisioned by the Holmes Group and Carnegie Forum reports, respectively. Even more directly, so does the network of professional development schools planned in Minnesota. According to Linda Darling-Hammond, that state soon will require new teachers to complete a one-year "internship" in one of these development schools. Each development school will be part of a local district and accredited for its special purpose by the state board of education. The cost of $10,000 per teacher is considered a small investment for the potential gain.[304]

There is an opportunity and a need in all these arrangements for substantial involvement not only of professional teacher organizations but of college and university faculty members, both in teacher education and the liberal arts. Higher education should strongly support them. They represent, potentially, the kind of partnership described by John Goodlad, "where two fundamentally different institutions (the universities and the schools) which must remain fundamentally different are joined for satisfaction of their overlapping self-interest."[305] Without strong programs of induction, campus efforts to put better teachers into the schools are often blunted—with a resulting waste of money, talent, and energy no one can afford.

The final component in the education of teachers is their continuing "in-service" training. Those who monitor state policy indicate that this has been little changed by school reform.[306] It should be. In-service education has been described as "private, eclectic, and diffuse" in character, a "patchwork collection of diverse activities" rather than a systematic program of professional development.[307] Much of it consists of "in-service days" featuring speeches by school administrators or workshops that carry college credit. (One teacher remarks, "It's more like buying credits than earning them.")[308]

When real college courses are selected—usually for certification or in-grade increments—current incentives tend to reward coursework in professional education rather than in a discipline.[309] Although knowledge is the currency in which the schools deal, keeping up with its growth—or expanding the breadth of one's holdings—is a luxury few teachers feel they can afford.[310]

States and local districts need to develop policies that reward teachers for further work and real mastery in their academic fields and support their efforts to renew their engagement with these disciplines. Colleges and universities need to provide appropriate and rigorous programs—either on the M.A.T. or M.A. and M.S. models—at times and prices that make them accessible to teachers. They also should work with local school districts to enrich in-service programs in the schools to focus them more on teachers' intellectual and academic development.

The most promising efforts to upgrade the continuing education of teachers so far have not originated with states, school boards, colleges, or universities. They are, instead, programs like the National Endowment for the Humanities Summer Seminars for School Teachers and the numerous voluntary associations—or "alliances"—of teachers, faculty members, and others that have emerged all around the country in the mid- and late-1980s. The Rockefeller Foundation, for example, has supported Collaboratives for Humanities and Arts Teaching (CHART), a national network of eleven partnerships. Located in nine cities (Atlanta, Los Angeles, New York, Philadelphia, Pittsburgh, San Francisco, Seattle, St. Louis, and St. Paul) and two states (Arkansas and South Carolina), CHART works to improve humanities and arts education in secondary schools "by focusing on teachers as the primary agents for change and reform in education."[311] It brings teachers together with colleagues from the schools, colleges, and cultural institutions to develop new curricula and improve teaching in the classroom.[312]

Like CHART, the Ford Foundation's Urban Mathematics Collaboratives focus on making teachers more knowledgeable about the subjects they teach—in this case, mathematics—and more resourceful in presenting them, especially in the inner-city high schools.[313] Encouraging communication and common study among university and secondary school teachers of history are aims of the History Teaching Alliance. This initiative of the American Historical Association, the National Council for Social Studies, and the Organization of American Historians operates in twenty states with sup-port from the President's Committee on the Arts and Humanities.[314]

These alliances and others like them serve not only to break down barriers between professional colleagues in the schools and colleges but to improve the quality of instruction at both levels. Those associated with these alliances speak about the "empowerment" felt by school teachers when they are recognized as professionals and the excitement these teachers feel as they renew their engagement with subjects they may have taught, but not really explored, for many years.

It is, of course, a perverse system of education that leaves its teachers hungry for intellectual experiences, not to mention professional respect. It is in higher education's power and interest to provide teachers with both these forms of sustenance, and in alliances it has an especially effective means of doing so.

THE ROLE OF THE STATES

Colleges and universities, finally, can undertake only the reforms that states allow. Too many states now specify the content of certification programs in terms of courses to be completed rather than competencies to be attained.[315] In doing so they deny institutions the freedom to take advantage of their particular strengths and find ways of covering particular topics and skills that may be far more efficient and productive than dedicated three-hour courses.[316]

As a part of the "first wave" of school reform, some states also have put limits on the total number of credit hours prospective teachers may take in education. These limits have obvious appeal, and in some states they have been a healthy corrective. Unfortunately, some states—such as Texas, with its ceiling of eighteen credits, including student teaching—have gone to counterproductive extremes. Legislators in such states are beginning to appreciate that they may have made it more difficult for colleges and universities to achieve programs of real quality.[317]

There are, by contrast, states in which colleges and universities have the latitude necessary to implement these steps. Massachusetts deregulated teacher education when it instituted certification testing, thereby allowing colleges and universities to determine how best to meet their goals.[318] More states should consider the advantages of deregulation: of holding higher education accountable for its product but giving it the freedom to determine the shape of its own programs.

Seasoned academic leaders know that some of the barriers to change frequently cited in higher educa-

tion—including regents' policies and accreditation standards—turn out as often as not to be mythical, or at least superable.[319] The external "barriers" to teacher education reform are no exception. The typical case is the state that specifies to a considerable extent the content and processes of teacher certification but nonetheless provides one route or another by which institutions can gain approval for nonconforming programs. It is telling that in most states, programs employing the strategies recommended here would have to be approved as "alternative" or "experimental" programs; we hope in time that they might become, and be recognized as, the norm.

Meanwhile, institutions should recognize that they may have more latitude for innovation now than they realize. As some programs in Chapter Ten illustrate, much can be accomplished even in oppressive regulatory settings by those who take a reasoned plan to state officials and negotiate for the freedom to implement it. As with other challenges posed in these pages, however, the prospects are likely to depend only partly on teacher educators. Effective involvement of those in the arts and sciences and in positions of institutional leadership is the best warrant for success.

CHAPTER EIGHT

EDUCATING MINORITY STUDENTS FOR TEACHING

THE MINORITY PIPELINE

STRATEGIC INTERVENTIONS

One of the "distributional" shortages of teachers the nation faces is a shortage of high-quality minority teachers. This shortage, already acute, will get worse in the near future and have distressing consequences for a nation committed to both quality and equality in education. The shortage, moreover, will be especially difficult to overcome: It is not just a function of changing patterns of interest or financing but reflects deeply rooted social and economic realities. This is not to say that changes made within the educational system cannot help. On the contrary, educational reforms can make a dramatic difference if they are sensitive to the dimensions of the problem and targeted at its causes.

There is, today, an imbalance between the number of minority students in this country and the number of minority teachers. Black children constitute 16 percent of the children in public schools and Hispanic children 9 percent.[320] Their numbers, moreover, soon will

While the percentage of minority
and "at-risk" children is large and growing,
the number of minority teachers is small
and almost certainly will diminish
over the remainder of the century

---

increase—both absolutely and in comparison with the number of white children. According to one recent—and relatively conservative—projection, the percentage of school-age minority children will reach 33 percent by the year 2000 and 39 percent by the year 2020.[321] Another study concludes, "By the year 2000, almost 42 percent of all American public school students will be minority children or other children living in poverty."[322]

While the percentage of school-age minority and "at-risk" children is large and growing, the number of minority teachers is small and almost certainly will diminish over the remainder of the century. Currently, only 6.9 percent of public school teachers are black and only 1.9 percent are Hispanic.[323] If current declines continue, by the early part of the next decade only about 5 percent of the nation's teachers will be drawn from minority groups.[324]

Because teaching positions require candidates to have a college education and typically are filled by graduates of teacher education programs, it is possible to estimate the future composition of the pool of teachers by looking at current trends in college enrollments generally and at enrollments in teacher education programs in particular. These figures show that there will not be enough black, Hispanic, Asian, and native

American teachers to replace the already dwindling number of practicing teachers from these groups.[325] Between 1976 and 1986, college enrollment among 18- to 24-year-old high school graduates dropped from 33 percent to 29 percent for blacks and from 36 percent to 29 percent for Hispanics. The figures for whites of the same age, meanwhile, went from 33 percent to 34 percent.[326]

The number of minority students preparing for careers in teaching already is small. For example, one study found that only 4.3 percent of the college enrollees preparing to teach in elementary schools and only 4.1 percent of those preparing to teach in the secondary schools are black.[327] Given these figures, the projection that minority teachers will constitute only 5 percent of the teaching force in the early 1990s does not seem unreasonable; it may even be optimistic. If it is accurate, it presents us with a picture of the future of American education in which "the average child, who has approximately forty teachers during his or her kindergarten through twelfth grade, can expect to have only two teachers from any minority."[328] Many, of course, will have none.

Increasing the number of minority teachers is essential to ensure the quality not just of the education of minority students—who need minority teachers as role models—but of all students. According to the American Association of Colleges for Teacher Education (AACTE), "A quality education requires that all students be exposed to the variety of cultural perspectives that represent the nation at large. Such exposure can be accomplished only via a multi-ethnic teaching force in which racial and ethnic groups are included at a level of parity with their numbers in the population."[329] Moreover, "the race and background of their teachers tells [students] something about authority and power in contemporary America. These messages influence children's attitudes toward school, their academic accomplishments, and their views of their own and others' intrinsic worth. The views they form in school about justice and fairness also influence their future citizenship."[330]

Why are there so few minority teachers? Problems in the teacher education pipeline cause a decline in minority participation at each successive level of educational attainment. For example, blacks constitute 17 percent of elementary and secondary school enrollments but represent only 10 percent of the college student population; they receive 7 percent of bachelor's degrees and only 4 percent of doctorates.[331] Let us examine more closely this educational pipeline and the fortunes of minority students in it.

THE MINORITY PIPELINE

Any discussion of the educational fortunes of minority students must begin with the social conditions in which many of these students find themselves before they enter school. Social and economic status is highly correlated with educational success: for example, school dropout rates are nearly three times as great for the poor as the nonpoor.[332] Many minority students, unfortunately, come from households at the lower end of the social and economic scale. Using 1986 data, *One-Third of a Nation* provides this documentation:

☐ Thirty-one percent of blacks and 27 percent of Hispanics have incomes below the poverty level.

☐ Median black family income is only 57 percent that of whites.

☐ The unemployment rate for blacks is 14 percent—more than twice the rate of 6 percent for whites.

☐ Minority parents are far less likely to have a college education. Twenty percent of whites over 25 have completed four years of college or more, versus 11 percent of blacks and only 8 percent of Hispanics.

☐ Health care for black children is substantially inferior to that for white children.

☐ The infant mortality rate for blacks is nearly twice as high as that for whites.[333]

Throughout the 1980s many of

those disparities have been getting worse. In short, minority students arrive at the schoolhouse door already "at-risk."

Poverty does not have to lead to long-term educational problems. The social and economic disadvantages suffered by many minority children, however, are compounded by institutionalized educational ones. We have mentioned that poor and minority students often are taught by less well-trained and experienced teachers than are children from more affluent families.[334] Their schools also tend to be underfunded, to have older physical plants, and to be more poorly supplied. Teachers at these schools are less likely to view their task as that of college preparation. These institutional disadvantages combine with social and economic disadvantages to put educational success out of reach for many minority students. As a result, minority students do not graduate at the same rate as white students. In 1986, for example, while 83 percent of white high school students finished high school, only 76 percent of black students and 60 percent of Hispanic students did so.[335]

The transition from high school to college—natural and inevitable to many from the white middle-class— can be extremely difficult for poor and minority children. For example, most four-year colleges require appli-cants to take the SAT. Minority students tend to do less well on this significant test than their white counterparts. In 1985, for example, 73 percent of the black students and 59 percent of the Hispanics taking the SAT scored below 400 on the verbal section; 64 percent of the blacks and 45 percent of the Hispanics scored below 400 on the math portion. Only 31 percent of the white students, on the other hand, had verbal scores below 400 and only 22 percent had math scores that low.[336]

Because minority students, on average, tend to come from poorer families, financial considerations more often cause them to forgo college. Many need either to seek employment immediately after finishing high school or to seek training that will quickly produce a saleable skill. Minority students constitute 32 percent of the enrollment in proprietary, business, and technical schools, and blacks represent 19 percent of active duty military forces.[337]

More than five million students are enrolled in the nation's twelve hundred community colleges. Among them are many of the minority and at-risk students who do pursue a higher education. More than 50 percent of Hispanic students and more than 40 percent of black students now in college are enrolled at the two-year level.[338] Moreover, according to data from the Cooperative Institutional Research Program (CIRP), between 1966 and 1987 the percentage of prospective teachers (white and minority) attending two-year institutions increased from 18 to 31 percent; the percentage remained constant for four-year institutions and declined for research universities.[339]

The emergence of two-year colleges as the growth sector in teacher education is problematic. Because two-year colleges cannot recommend students for certification, students who wish to pursue a career in teaching eventually must transfer to a four-year college, which often is difficult. "Transferring...from two- to four-year colleges—and potentially into teacher education programs—is stifled by poor articulation, or coordination, of course credits between the two types of institutions and by a lack of financial resources and/or incentives for the students."[340] Furthermore, since many teacher education programs still require a relatively sequential course of study that cannot be begun at two-year colleges, students who enter two-year colleges aspiring to teach often face a prohibitively long and expensive program.

Minority and at-risk students who enter four-year colleges are less likely to graduate than their majority peers. According to *High School and Beyond*, the Department of Education's national longitudinal study of

the high school class of 1972, 45 percent of all students who entered public four-year colleges and 52 percent of all students who entered independent institutions received their bachelor's degree within six years of entry. By contrast, only 26 percent of black and Hispanic students graduated within the same period.[341]

Since most prospective teachers—majority and minority—traditionally have taken their college degrees in education, the number taking such degrees gives us a fair index of interest in the career. The degrees minority students receive now are less likely to be in education than before. Between 1975 and 1985, the number of minority students graduating with bachelor's degrees in education fell by more than 50 percent.[342]

One apparent reason for this change, in addition to increased opportunities in other fields and a drop in the public and parental support given to students who are considering teaching, has been the testing of teachers. An increasing number of states are requiring individuals to pass admissions tests before entering teacher education programs and competency tests before being certified as teachers. In 1988, for example, 25 states required standardized tests for admission to teacher education programs in higher education institutions, while 34 states required standardized certification tests for new teachers. The use of these tests has greatly reduced the number of minority students entering the field. According to AACTE, "average pass rates for [admission tests and certification tests] are approximately 72 percent and 83 percent, respectively. For minorities, [however,] the pass rates are much lower; for example, during 1984–85, only 23 percent of blacks and 34 percent of Hispanics passed the Texas admission test. On teacher certification tests, Alabama had pass rates of 15 percent for blacks and 78 percent for whites, while Florida had pass rates of 37 percent for blacks and 92 percent for whites."[343] Approximately fifteen to twenty thousand minority students have failed such tests each year.[344] These high failure rates have discouraged minority students from pursuing careers in education.

Three other points in the minority teacher education pipeline deserve mention. The first is the point of entry into a teaching career: In some areas school districts may not be doing all they can to hire minority teachers. Second, minority teachers who are hired sometimes find it more difficult to advance, in part because advancing one's career often requires obtaining an advanced degree at additional expense. Third, it is often difficult to retain minority teachers. According to a recent Harris poll, 41

percent of black and Hispanic teachers surveyed, as compared to 25 percent of white teachers, indicate that they would probably leave teaching in the next five years. Minority teachers who were considering a change of career included more than half of those who have taught for less than five years. The most frequently cited reasons for leaving the field were relatively low salaries and lack of meaningful involvement in decisions that affect their working conditions, but these teachers also indicated that the pressures to switch careers had grown as opportunities for minorities in other, more lucrative, fields have opened up.[345]

The future supply of minority teachers depends on the number of minority teacher candidates in the pipeline today. Unfortunately, while there is no shortage of minority children who might become good teachers, the teacher education pipeline often fails to deliver them to the profession.

STRATEGIC INTERVENTIONS

We have argued elsewhere in this volume—and reemphasize here—that four-year integrated programs that recruit and prepare liberal arts majors might be the most effective means of increasing the number and quality of both minority and nonminority teachers. In this section, however, we will consider a number of other reforms, including some that are narrowly focused on improving existing teacher education programs.

Precollege programs

At the earliest stages of the pipeline—preschool to ninth grade—the task of producing more and higher quality minority teachers is identical with that of improving the social and economic status of minority families and improving education for minority children. Programs that upgrade schools, aid families in raising their children, or give students special help have an important role to play. It is essential that society maintain and expand programs such as Head Start and Upward Bound and invest in programs to upgrade inner-city or other predominantly minority schools, both at the elementary and secondary levels.

Some of these programs can involve minority high school and college students in ways that help channel them toward careers in education. One promising program aimed at minority children at the high school level has been in operation for four years at Coolidge High School in Washington, D.C. In this "Teaching Professions Program," high school students recruited in their first or second year take a special program consisting of standard academic work supplemented with special classes—in education, speech, computers, and the humanities—designed to introduce them to the fundamentals of education while preparing them for college work. As seniors, participants are required to visit a city public school regularly and assist a full-time teacher. If they successfully complete this program, they are not only prepared for college but they already have some exposure to teaching. Moreover, if they agree to teach at least three years in the District of Columbia public school system, they will be guaranteed substantial financial aid for college.[346]

This program simultaneously addresses several of the problems in the minority teacher education pipeline: First, it helps improve the education of minority children at the elementary schools to which the assistants are assigned. Second, because of its emphasis on college preparation, it makes the curricula of participating minority students less vocational and more academic. Finally, because it pays the college tuition of the graduates, it makes college a real possibility for at least some students.

Recruitment

Direct recruitment of high school students is perhaps the simplest way to increase the number and quality of both minority and nonminority students preparing to teach. Findings like those from a recent survey of high school sophomores show how much work is to be done and how early the effort must start. Although only tenth graders, the students surveyed already rated teaching "very low" among possible careers. Regardless of race, gender, or school location, most "'loathed' teaching as a career alternative—especially those in advanced classes."[347]

With their easy access to the schools, teacher education faculty members already have an enormous and unexploited advantage. By using their access to make a case for teaching, they might be able to combat many of the social forces that turn students away from this career. They can speak in classrooms, assemblies, and other school forums. They can distribute literature to students. They can work with high school principals, teachers, and counselors to identify students interested in teaching. All these professionals can work together to support appropriate preprofessional experience for interested high school students: They can, for example, provide service and tutoring opportunities, encourage the formation of student preprofessional organizations, and provide opportunities for on-campus study.

The Minority Teacher Preparation program at the University of Wis-consin–Whitewater exemplifies some of these strategies. It seeks to increase the number of minority teacher education students by working through high school academic advisors to identify and aggressively recruit qualified students. The program also has other points of focus, however: It attempts to recruit community college students through improved advising, priority registration, and guaranteed enrollment at the university, and it tries to identify students already on campus who might, with some encouragement, enroll in the teacher education program. The program gives encouragement in the form of special scholarships, tutorial help, and special advising and counseling. It also attempts to provide a "support community" of sympathetic faculty members and other students to ease the adjustment to campus life. Total minority student enrollments in education at Whitewater still are small, but as a result of the program they have more than doubled.

Educational partnerships

Directly recruiting minority students will increase the number of minority students attending four-year colleges, but it will do little by itself to attack the structural problems that cause most of them to receive poor academic preparation. Unless four-year colleges can do more to improve the primary and secondary school education of minority students generally, they will condemn these students to a second-rate education and themselves to endless competition for a small number of qualified minority student candidates. Stepped-up efforts in the schools, including formal school-college partnerships, are not options so much as they are prerequisites to progress in this area. Educational partnerships with local schools are an increasingly common and potentially very powerful means of change.

A variety of partnerships is possible, involving a range of commitments on the part of higher education. Some school-college partnerships are directed at recruitment. One is the "Teaching Opportunities Program for Students" developed at Temple University. Interested students at two participating high schools are given the opportunity to join "clubs" advised by two teachers from the schools. Club members tutor in their own schools, assist in the classroom, visit other schools to observe special teaching programs, and audit classes at Temple. After graduating from high school, those students who meet Temple's entrance requirements can enroll in a bachelors program in the College of Arts and Sciences while completing certification requirements in the College of Education. Students who teach in the Philadelphia

school system for five years will qualify for a loan-forgiveness program.

Heritage College and the Yakima, Washington, school district have developed a program to recruit persons not currently enrolled in school. This program attempts to interest nonacademic—and in most cases Hispanic—staff members of the school district in a special teacher training program for bilingual teachers at the college. The two institutions jointly developed the curriculum so that it would meet both state teaching requirements and the needs of the district. Classes are given at times that are convenient to the staff, while facilities are provided by the district. The financial burden is borne by both institutions. The program is designed so that the participants can complete a degree in three years without forgoing their pre-enrollment incomes. In effect, the program extends the career ladder of the district's nonacademic staff. It is expected that, as a result of the program, the district's minority teaching staff will double in the program's first four years.

School-college partnerships can be much more sophisticated, and they can be aimed at more than improved recruitment. In 1974, LaGuardia Community College of the City University of New York opened Middle College, the first collaborative high school/college pro-

Colleges and universities can improve
the quality of education at local schools
by offering cooperative programs that
focus on the professional needs of teachers

gram for at-risk students. The school enrolls students who are identified as high-risk students with college potential. It encourages them to succeed by providing them with role models, small classes, and enriched academic and support services. Because Middle College is located on LaGuardia's campus, its students are surrounded by successful peer models—the LaGuardia students— and have access to LaGuardia's academic support services. High school students also can participate in a number of LaGuardia's academic programs, including its cooperative education program. Despite the "high-risk" nature of the student body, about 85 percent graduate. Of these, 75 percent go on to college— many of them to LaGuardia.[348]

Davidson College has entered into a partnership with the Charlotte-Mecklenburg, North Carolina, school system that is designed to increase the number of black high school graduates who are prepared for the academic rigors of selective colleges and universities and explore ways in which predominantly white educational institutions can be more supportive of minority college students. Each year, Davidson and the school district select thirty black eighth-grade students with underdeveloped potential to participate in a five-year sequential program of academic-year and summer experi-

ences that takes the participants through their first year of college. The program focuses on three academic areas (English, math, and science), test-taking skills, and personal development. The academic programs aim to help students qualify for the advanced college preparatory courses in their high schools. The summer programs were designed in consultation with high school teachers and with a special emphasis on the needs and interests of black high school students; they include classes in test-taking strategies and in physical fitness and "wellness" (including coursework designed to inform students about drug use and sexuality and to help raise their self-image). In time, there will be a substantial evaluation of the program. Although long-term results are not yet available, a 1987 study of the initial group of students participating in this program found that they registered a statistically significant improvement in their SAT math scores.

The Philadelphia Schools Collaborative Project makes use of educational partnerships to help radically restructure predominantly minority "comprehensive" high schools. Funded by the Pew Memorial Trust, this program seeks to revive inner-city high school education by breaking large and relatively impersonal schools into smaller "houses" or "schools-within-schools," each specializing in a particular subject. By creating relatively intimate learning communities and allowing faculty members and administrators the autonomy to implement experimental programs, project leaders hope to create a social and educational environment that can reduce a nearly 50 percent dropout rate. A task force of admissions officers from local colleges and universities has been formed to promote recruitment from the restructured schools. Information about the colleges will be made available, and the colleges will help the schools improve and expand their academic advising.

Project leaders also hope to expand, integrate, and improve collaborative efforts already in place. For example, the University of Pennsylvania's large tutoring program—which has given more than three hundred college students the opportunity to tutor minority children—might be incorporated into the programs that Temple University has developed with the schools of north Philadelphia. The large scale of the project and the autonomy of the individual houses will make it possible to develop a variety of partnership projects, ranging from a small experimental program at one house involving only a few faculty members to a citywide project involving many colleges.

Increasingly, colleges and universities are finding that "adopting" an existing school is a relatively easy way of developing collaborative relationships with local school districts. Adoptions make possible a variety of interactions and can be tailored to fit the needs of the school and the resources of the university. Institutions can, for example, share facilities, exchange faculty members, assist in job placement and recruiting, develop special academic programs, and assist one another with counseling and articulation.

Augusta College, in Augusta, Georgia, has adopted two predominantly minority local schools, Lamar Elementary School and Laney High School. At Lamar, Augusta's students run a tutoring program, while Augusta faculty members conduct staff development workshops. Augusta supervises more than twenty programs at Laney High, including workshops on computers and special classes in political science. In cooperation with the NAACP, Augusta has sponsored a series of lectures for high school students that are given by black professionals.[349] Adoptions such as this allow both institutions the administrative flexibility to respond to a range of needs.

Finally, colleges and universities can improve the quality of education at local schools by offering cooperative programs that focus on the professional needs of teachers. The quality of education that students receive depends, in large part, on the continuing education of teachers. Such "in-service" training programs can range from those designed to create "communities of scholars" within academic disciplines; to centers for professional development; to colloquia, summer institutes, and special degree programs.[350] These kinds of programs, some of which were discussed in Chapter Seven, offer colleges and universities the opportunity to improve local schools without requiring the degree of involvement demanded by adopt-a-school programs.

Articulation between two-year and four-year institutions

As we have seen, two-year colleges are vitally important points of access for minorities entering higher education. The most important thing that two-year colleges can do to improve educational success—for both white and minority students generally and for prospective teachers in particular—is to enter into relationships with four-year colleges to ease and increase the transfer of students between the two types of institutions. A special concern is the transferability of general-education credit.

Two-year colleges also must begin to offer programs of study that will allow students to transfer directly into the junior year of teacher education programs at four-year colleges. Improving recruiting and advising at the two-year colleges would be an essential part of any such effort. The success of several current collaborations—such as that of Pace University with Westchester Community College—demonstrates that such comprehensive programs can work.[351]

Improving teacher education programs

Successful college-level programs must do more than help minority students graduate from high school, and they must do more than aggressively recruit those minority students. They also must graduate the students they recruit.

Much can be done at four-year colleges to ensure the graduation of more and better prepared minority teachers. It is essential that the financial problems many minority students face be addressed. It is necessary also to overcome the social attitudes—most importantly, widespread indifference to social justice and the economic tensions caused by affirmative action programs—that have made the campus climate for minorities increasingly chilly in recent years. At a time when some refer to a "new racism on campus," it is essential that academic communities decrease racial tension and promote cross-cultural understanding and the acceptance of diversity.[352]

Administrators and faculty members must take specific actions to ensure that minority students achieve educational success. Traditional programs seek to help minority students develop better study skills or give remedial assistance to help minority students overcome poor subject matter preparation. Uri Treisman, founder of the Mathematics Workshop Program at the University of California–Berkeley, has developed a different approach. Basing his views on the research he conducted on factors correlated with the academic success of black math students at Berkeley, Treisman disputes the assumptions used to justify traditional remedial programs.

Black students do poorly in math courses, Treisman's research shows, not because they are poorly motivated or poorly prepared but because they are isolated from their instructors and their classmates. His program to help black students learn calculus emphasizes three points: students must learn to excel, not just avoid failure; they must work in collaborative learning situations, not independently; and they must work directly with the math faculty, rather than with special tutors. Treisman's program shows that minority students can achieve academic success without remedial training if they are encouraged to take on intellectually challenging work in a support-ive social environment.

Improving minority recruitment and graduation rates also will require finding alternatives to the extension of teacher education programs over periods of five or more years. In the words of Reginald Wilson and Deborah Carter, "adding a year to the study required for entering the profession will cause disproportionate economic hardship for minority students. For many, education will cease to be a viable career."[349] If we are to increase the quality and number of minority teachers, we must work within the four-year framework already in place at many colleges and universities.

Successful programs also must ensure that a large proportion of their graduates pass teacher certification tests. In response to an 82 percent failure rate on Florida's newly instituted four-part teacher certification examination, Bethune-Cookman College, a predominantly black college, developed its Teacher Education Institute (TEI). The institute's purpose is to develop innovative approaches to the recruitment, retention, and professional development of the college's students. It brings together teams of education students and faculty members from both education and the liberal arts to supplement the regular advising system. Team members visit local schools to learn about education and to recruit.

They also sponsor discussions and formal seminars. Other aspects of the program include special financial aid supplement packages, an honors program, and special tutoring by liberal arts faculty members in subjects likely to appear on certification exams. According to the former director of the TEI program, 100 percent of the Bethune-Cookman students taking the Florida certification exam during the first two years of the program passed.

Because only 10 percent of its students were passing the Louisiana teacher certification test, Grambling University implemented a program designed to improve students' performance. Today, 99 percent of Grambling's students pass. Central to this improvement was a revision of its curriculum undertaken with the help of the Educational Testing Service (ETS). Consultants from ETS were able to pinpoint several weaknesses in the performance of Grambling's students on the National Teacher Examination—in particular, difficulties on questions that test general knowledge. Grambling's curricular reform, therefore, has focused on improving general education. Education students are required to have a concentration in an academic field, usually in the liberal arts. Students also are offered special workshops in mathematics and in writing. As a result of this program, the number of graduates of Grambling's education program who are certified to teach has increased significantly, even though the total number of graduates has fallen.[354]

The Bethune-Cookman and Grambling programs might be criticized for "teaching the tests." This criticism misses the mark on two counts, however. The emphasis is on increasing the amount of time students spend on "content areas"; thus students receive a better—that is, a broader and deeper—education in the arts and sciences. Second, to the extent that any "test-teaching" occurs, it may actually be appropriate. As Wilson and Melendez have pointed out, "Any requirements for additional and more rigorous tests should be accompanied by strategies and resources to increase the pass rates of minorities."[355]

Moreover, while teaching tests does little directly to improve the quality of the minority teaching pool, it may do this indirectly by helping to overcome one choke point in the minority teacher education pipeline. The rates at which minority students fail certification exams generally are known to those who are considering a career in teaching, and they are cited often by minority students who choose not to pursue this option as a reason for their decision. To the extent that teaching the tests raises the rates at which minority students pass these examinations, it might encourage qualified minority students who are now afraid to consider a career in education.

Integrating liberal arts and education

Many of these programs aim at recruiting more minority students into colleges of education and/or aiding the students in those departments to become teachers. The declining numbers of minority students majoring in education and their generally low academic profile make it unlikely, however, that the solution to the shortage of high-quality minority teachers will be found in such reforms alone. As we have argued in previous chapters, to find a group of academically talented minority students large enough to meet the nation's needs we must look beyond the colleges of education to the arts and sciences.

Again, the numbers tell the story. In 1985, the number of black students who received degrees in the arts and sciences was nearly three-and-a-half times the number of black students who received degrees in education, while graduating Hispanic arts and sciences students outnumbered their counterparts in education by nearly four to one. More importantly, members of particular demographic subgroups, such as

black males—who are particularly underrepresented in the teaching profession—are much more likely to receive degrees in the arts and sciences than in education. In 1985, for example, black males graduated from arts and sciences programs at five times the rate that they graduated from education.[356] Bringing only a fraction of these individuals into the kinds of programs described in the body of this text would substantially increase the number of teachers from underrepresented minority groups.

In addition to being more numerous, minority students majoring in the arts and sciences are, on average and as measured by standardized tests, generally more talented academically than their counterparts in the colleges of education. For example, in 1987, while the average combined SAT score for black males intending to major in education was 635, for black males intending to major in the humanities it was 831. For black females intending to major in education the average was 666, while those intending to major in the humanities averaged 837. Generally speaking, among minority students prospective arts and sciences majors outscored prospective education majors by about 20 percent.[357] Care always should be exercised in comparing SAT scores; these statistics, however, do compare scores of similar racial and sexual groups. These results also are reinforced by the students' reports of their rank in high-school classes. The self-reported rank of black students intending to major in education was about 10 percent lower than that of black students intending to enter the arts and sciences.[358]

The key to increasing the numbers of minority teachers lies in collectively employing an array of strategies—both the recruitment of minority liberal arts majors into four-year integrated programs and the kinds of programs described earlier in this chapter. All of these approaches can help, but the first steps—which we hope this review will help foster—are the same for all individuals and institutions, no matter what means they choose to adopt: We need to recognize that the problem is extremely serious, and we must determine to do something about it.

A SURVEY OF CERTIFICATION PROGRAMS

In 1987 AAC sought information about the ways U.S. colleges and universities attract undergraduate arts and sciences majors to teaching and prepare them for it. Never before collected, this information provides a baseline against which future efforts can be measured. It also helps instruct us as to the shape such efforts might take.

With assistance from the project advisory committee and several consultants, AAC designed a questionnaire that was sent in May 1987 to the 1,378 U.S. colleges and universities granting baccalaureate degrees in the arts and sciences.[359] By the end of August 1987, 804 institutions (58 percent of those targeted) had responded to our survey. Of these institutions, 601 (75 percent) reported having an institutional program or process by which arts and sciences

majors can be prepared to teach within the traditional four-year context.

The survey results provide the first basic descriptive profile of these 601 programs: information, for example, on their numbers, locations, enrollments, administrative structures, and requirements. The data do not support judgments as to which programs are "best" or "most successful" or "most effective." They do give us a reasonable basis, however, for categorizing programs by what we call their "program viability." As a result, we are able to identify some characteristics that distinguish stronger from weaker programs.

Several survey questions, for example, solicited information on enrollment trends, absolute and relative program size, and absolute and relative student ability levels. Using a

Viable certification processes
for arts and sciences majors
are likely to be found
in association with education units
structured in a variety of different ways

weighted scheme to award points for different answers to these questions, we divided the 601 schools into three "tiers"—essentially a top 20 percent, a middle 60 percent, and a bottom 20 percent.[360] We then were able to compare the responses of different tiers and isolate those questions on which, by formal tests of statistical significance, their answers differed.

In reporting our data, we cite medians rather than averages; the former are less prone to skewing by data extremes and are, for our purposes, more descriptive. When we report a percentage, it indicates the percentage of all schools responding to a particular question. The data we report are for the academic year 1986–87 unless 1985–86 is specified.

Accompanying the questionnaire was a cover letter requesting that the survey be forwarded to "the individual on [your] campus who is responsible for the process by which undergraduates currently majoring in the arts and sciences can pursue teacher certification." Individuals completing the questionnaire held various positions. Some were arts and sciences faculty members or administrators; some were education faculty members or administrators; still others spanned both worlds and held joint appointments. The majority, however, were affiliated with schools or departments of education. To the extent the results are biased, therefore,

they most likely are biased toward the views of teacher educators.

Initial survey questions gathered general information about the 601 institutions reporting that they have a process by which arts and sciences majors can be certified to teach. Sixty-two percent of these schools are private and 38 percent are public. These percentages mirror the 64 percent/36 percent ratio nationwide of private versus public baccalaureate-granting colleges and universities. The private/public ratio did not differ significantly across our three tiers, suggesting that more viable programs are no more likely to be found in institutions under one form of control than the other. Virtually all (99 percent) of the 601 institutions are regionally accredited. Our median institution enrolled 2,077 undergraduates and, in 1985–86, awarded 416 baccalaureate degrees, of which 230 were in the arts and sciences.

We turn next to questions about the kinds of programs through which these institutions prepare teachers. Of the 601 colleges and universities with programs to prepare arts and sciences majors to teach, 475 (79 percent) indicated that they also grant baccalaureate degrees in education; the remaining 126 (21 percent) indicated that an arts and sciences degree plus teacher education coursework was their sole path to teacher certification. Those institutions in our sample that award education degrees conferred a median number of twenty-five of them in 1985–86, a number representing approximately 6 percent of all their baccalaureate degrees. While 90 percent of these institutions offered degrees in elementary education, 54 percent offered secondary education degrees and 50 percent offered both. However, 40 percent offered only elementary education degrees, and 3 percent offered only secondary education degrees.

At three-quarters of the 601 schools, teacher education is organized as either a department offering a major in education (42 percent) or a school or college of education (32 percent). The percentage of institutions organizing teacher education in these and other kinds of units was essentially the same across the tiers. Thus, viable certification processes for arts and sciences majors are likely to be found in association with education units structured in a variety of different ways. Half of the schools, colleges, departments, and programs of education have (48 percent) or have pending (2 percent) NCATE accreditation, and nearly all (98 percent, with 1 percent pending) have state-approved teacher preparation programs.

Institutions provided information about enrollments in their teacher preparation programs for arts and sciences majors and the levels of certification offered. While 63 percent were able to offer both elementary and secondary certification processes, 36 percent offered secondary only and 1 percent offered elementary only. One significant finding was that upper-tier schools disproportionately offer both secondary and elementary certification.

When queried about enrollment trends in these programs for arts and sciences majors, 47 percent of responding schools reported enrollments holding steady, and 30 percent reported them increasing over the last four years. Only 14 percent of the 601 institutions reported declines in program enrollments. With more than three of every four of these programs enjoying either steady or increasing enrollments, it would seem that these kinds of programs are serving a need.[361]

To determine the arts and sciences fields from which the 601 programs draw students, the survey asked about the representation of different types of arts and sciences majors within them. Of the responding institutions, 69 percent reported that humanities majors were enrolled in numbers proportionate to their representation in the pool of all undergraduate arts and sciences majors. Only 24 percent of institutions reported that humanities majors were underrepresented. Fifty-nine percent of schools reported proportional representation of social science majors, with only 21 percent citing underrepresentation. Fine arts majors and math/science majors, however, were nearly as likely to be underrepresented (47 percent and 48 percent, respectively) as they were to be proportionally represented (49 percent and 48 percent, respectively.)

On the whole, although almost all schools report unequal proportions in the math/science area, upper-tier schools were more apt to report proportional representation across the arts and sciences disciplines than were those in the lower tier. This result may suggest that more viable programs also tend to make themselves better known and more accessible to students in all the major domains of the arts and sciences and may secure the cooperation and support of a broader range of faculty members.

A key survey question concerned the number of minority arts and sciences majors recommended for certification during 1985–86. To our disappointment, 60 percent of our 601 institutions either did not answer the question or reported "none." This response—the survey equivalent of an awkward silence— suggests lax recordkeeping or, where information is available, the existence of nothing to report. It sug-

gests how few of the programs have begun seriously to address themselves to the shortage of minority teachers.

Another set of survey questions sought information about the academic ability of arts and sciences majors seeking teacher certification. A healthy majority (68 percent) of respondents rated them equal in academic ability to education majors (a result that one may wish to evaluate in light of the predominance of education faculty members and administrators among the respondents). Where a difference was perceived, it was far more often in favor of the arts and sciences majors pursuing certification. Using standardized test scores as a measure, 15 percent rated the arts and sciences majors academically superior, while only 1 percent rated the education majors academically more able. Asked to use grade point average as a measure of academic ability, 71 percent of respondents rated the two groups the same. Again, where a difference was observed, arts and sciences majors were usually thought to be more able: Twelve percent of respondents said arts and sciences majors had higher GPAs; 3 percent made that claim for education majors.

These results would seem to support the contention that, if anything, arts and sciences majors preparing to be teachers constitute a relatively able pool and are thought to be so even by the teacher educators responding to our survey. While these ability ratings were not significant across our tiers, upper-tier school respondents were far more likely to express an opinion on this question, perhaps indicating that more viable programs do a better job of collecting information on which to base an opinion.

The questionnaire also asked respondents to compare the academic ability of arts and sciences majors seeking teacher certification with that of arts and sciences majors not seeking teacher certification. Again, standardized test scores and GPAs were used as measures. Neither group emerged as stronger by either indicator—73 percent of our respondents reported that the two groups' test scores were approximately the same, 6 percent attributed higher scores to arts and sciences students pursuing teacher certification, and 6 percent did so to arts and sciences students not pursuing teacher certification. The results using GPAs as a measure were similar: 71 percent, 12 percent, and 5 percent, respectively. Again, where there was a difference, it favored arts and sciences majors pursuing certification.[362] Some may see in this result a tendency on the part of the teacher educator respondents to exaggerate the strengths of the liberal arts majors perceptive

enough to seek out certification programs. Others may think it supports contentions that liberal arts majors preparing for teaching really are, as a group, at least as able as their arts and sciences peers.

The survey also sought some basic comparative information about the attitudes and interests of the two groups of arts and sciences majors. We tested a number of points of common wisdom in this regard and found that they held up well. One half or more of all respondents rated arts and sciences majors seeking certification as having more career direction, more interest in service careers and working with young people, and less concern with salary than their arts and sciences counterparts who are not seeking certification. Encouragingly, 72 percent of the respondents viewed both groups as having equal interest in their academic major.

A substantial set of questions explored the nature of special recruitment efforts and scheduling and advising arrangements for arts and sciences majors preparing to teach. Asked whether these students could complete both degree and certification requirements in eight semesters (or its equivalent in quarters, trimesters, etc.) without an overload, 79 percent of responding institutions answered "yes," although a fair number went on to qualify or even technically disqualify their answers. Responses to this question differed significantly by tier: upper- and middle-tier schools were much more likely to respond affirmatively.

We then asked schools if they make a special effort to schedule teacher education courses so that they will be accessible to arts and sciences majors. Eighty-three percent reported that they do, most often by scheduling education courses during the regular academic year so as to minimize conflict with courses required of arts and sciences majors and by offering education courses during the summer.

Institutions use several strategies to alert arts and sciences majors to the option of teacher certification: 99 percent use formal academic advising; 98 percent, their catalogue; 75 percent, presentations to student groups; and 47 percent, mailings. The two methods rated "highly effective" by the largest number of respondents are formal academic advising (46 percent) and informal academic advising (39 percent). Differences in the rating of these two methods also were significant across tiers: upper-tier schools were disproportionately likely to rate them "highly effective."

AAC also wished to find out how the person responsible for the certification program for arts and sciences students usually is alerted to a student's interest in teaching. Essentially, we wanted to know what types of "early warning systems" such programs have in place to detect a student's emerging interest and preliminary explorations in education. A student's seeking an interview with a member of the education faculty was cited by 73 percent as a point of alert. Two-thirds said they would notice when a student enrolls in an introductory education course, and an equal percentage responded they would know when the student informs his or her regular academic advisor. Another 58 percent cited the point at which the student would make formal application to a program.

Of the four choices offered to respondents, each was checked by between 58 percent and 73 percent; the modal response was to check a combination of three, and more than 25 percent checked all four methods. Although most institutions therefore seem to have their figurative antennae out, upper- and middle-tier schools were more apt to detect incipient student interest in teaching through monitoring of introductory education course enrollments. Noting interest through formal application to a program also was an upper-tier characteristic. Here, too, initiative and the use of formal procedures distinguish the more viable programs.

Information provided about the sources of academic advising for arts and sciences majors pursuing teacher certification was similarly revealing. Of responding institutions, 76 percent indicated that such students have a regular arts and sciences faculty advisor in addition to a regular teacher education faculty advisor. Upper-tier institutions were disproportionately apt to provide an arts and sciences advisor especially for arts and sciences majors interested in teaching or to provide these students a combination of regular arts and sciences advisor and special teacher education faculty advisor. The upper-tier characteristic in this case, therefore, is a specially designated advisor—either from the arts and sciences, teacher education, or both.

We turn now to issues of governance and of faculty members' and administrators' awareness of, and involvement in, these programs for arts and sciences majors. Asked how programs are administered, 66 percent of responding institutions indicated that the head of teacher education plans, oversees, and coordinates the process by which arts and sciences majors are prepared to teach. A minority within each tier reported that two persons, one each from education and the arts and sciences, shared responsibility for this program, with upper-tier respondents constituting the largest group reporting this arrangement.

A large majority of respondents (86 percent) describe most arts and sciences administrators as aware of their programs. Fewer (76 percent) claim that their programs are known to most liberal arts faculty members, and lower-tier schools were the least likely of all, by a significant margin, to report more than "a few" faculty members and administrators aware of their programs. These findings confirm that there is room for improvement in an area—building an awareness of the program on campus—in which relatively easy gains are to be had.

Rated as "very supportive" of the efforts made by arts and sciences majors to pursue teacher certification were 90 percent of teacher education faculty members, 86 percent of teacher education administrators, 53 percent of arts and sciences administrators, 49 percent of math/science faculty members, 44 percent of social science faculty members, 40 percent of humanities faculty members, and 39 percent of fine arts faculty members. The respondents—teacher educators themselves in most cases—clearly do not credit the claim that faculty members and administrators in their field are impediments to arts and sciences majors wishing to teach. Since supportiveness on the part of teacher educators was considerably weaker, however, among

Education programs have not convinced
academic policymakers that their courses
are broadly educative and might have
a place in the curriculum of any student

lower-tier institutions, it emerges
clearly as a critical variable.

There is the suggestion, in the relatively high marks given to math
and science faculty members for supportiveness, that faculty members in
different liberal arts disciplines are
not equally likely to discourage their
strong students from pursuing an interest in teaching. Although at least
some professors in every field may
actively support students interested
in teaching, students may hear the
traditional, chilling confidence,
"You're much too good for that," in
some fields of study more than in
others.

According to the respondents, one
or more arts and sciences faculty
members are at least moderately involved in the following activities associated with the program preparing
arts and sciences majors to teach: on
an advisory committee (in 84 percent
of such programs), in team teaching
(65 percent), in collaborative efforts
with elementary and secondary
school teachers (61 percent), in supervising student teachers (59 percent), or in program administration
(53 percent). Indeed, in each tier,
more than half of the respondents
indicate at least moderate arts and
sciences faculty involvement in all
these areas—a foundation, it would
seem, on which to build further cooperative efforts.

The AAC survey sought to identify
the courses and exposures to areas of
coverage that state authorities or
program administrators require for
certification. At least 75 percent of
all responding institutions require
work in twelve areas for elementary
certification: introduction to education, foundations, human development, general methods, methods in
math, methods in science, methods
in language arts, methods in social
studies, teaching of reading, special
education, pre-student teaching field
experience, and student teaching.
For prospective secondary teachers
in at least 75 percent of responding
institutions, coverage of eight areas
is required. These students substitute
one methods course in a content
area for the four separate special
methods courses in math, science,
language arts and social studies, and
they need not complete the work in
special education required for elementary certification. Otherwise, the
eight areas required by the great majority of survey respondents are the
same for secondary as for elementary
certification.

A central concern was to determine respondents' views regarding
the extent of liberal and general education provided by education courses
required for teacher certification.
Asked which three required education courses "best provide significant
liberal as well as professional education," the respondents named the

following courses: foundations (listed by approximately 80 percent), human development (54 percent), introduction to education (35 percent), general methods (approximately 12 percent), and methods in a content area (approximately 9 percent).

Our next question—asking in which education courses required for teacher certification it would be beneficial for liberal education to have a more central role—elicited notably little response. More than half (54 percent) of respondents failed to list a single course required for elementary certification; 49 percent listed nothing required for secondary. This result, or lack of one, suggests a reluctance on the part of teacher educators to wrestle with the kinds of questions being asked of their profession: central questions about how their offerings—all of them—can be made better vehicles for liberal learning. Those who did answer seemed disinclined to think about new possibilities, listing the same courses they had said best provide liberal education.

Our evidence, in short, suggests that even in these programs for arts and sciences majors, liberal education too often is left to the liberal arts and a few introductory and foundations courses. The kind of thinking that will be necessary to change this situation seems, in most programs, not to be going on.

We conclude this summary by reporting an equally revealing response to our inquiry about the part played by education courses in each institution's general-education program. In contrast to the preceding question, this one prompted a 98 percent response, and the answers add up to a clear challenge. Only 36 percent of institutions report having even one education course that counts toward the fulfillment of general education requirements. This fact goes far toward explaining the intellectual isolation and recruiting difficulty facing teacher education programs. Education programs have not done the work they need to do in order to convince curriculum committees and other academic policymakers that their courses are broadly educative and might have a place in the curriculum of any student. As a result, in most settings education is not a player in the great competition for students' minds and interests that general education largely represents.

In sum, we have found that most U.S. colleges and universities have a certification process or program for liberal arts majors—and hence a basic programmatic framework for many of the kinds of changes recommended in this volume. These programs attract good students from all arts and sciences disciplines and meet a real, if not yet great, demand.

In general, the more viable programs are relatively formalized. They are aware of themselves as entities; they are "programs" rather than merely "processes." They are actively managed and widely known and supported on campus. They make especially effective use of formal and informal academic advising and special efforts to coordinate the scheduling of arts and sciences and education courses. They are more likely than other programs to enable students to complete arts and sciences degree requirements in eight semesters, and students pursuing this route to teaching are more likely to enjoy the full support of education faculty members.

If these findings about the practices of top-tier programs suggest directions in which future efforts can point, other findings about the whole population of programs highlight obvious areas of underachievement. They suggest ample room for improvement and many opportunities yet to be seized. Teacher educators seem not to be attending to the representation of minority students. They are doing little thinking about how their programs can be vehicles of liberal education. And they have not developed broad general-education courses to interest arts and sciences students in their field. Because so little has been done in these areas, even modest efforts may produce gratifying results.

INNOVATIVE PROGRAMS

Programs on numerous campuses around the country illustrate how the strategies recommended in this volume can work—and are working—to strengthen the undergraduate preparation of teachers. This chapter features eleven such programs, at institutions public and private, large and small, in nine different states in several regions. Some of these institutions are highly selective, others less so. Some have extensive graduate programs, others none. Their certification programs exemplify a common concern, however, with strengthening themselves through the integration of professional education and the liberal arts and with bringing students of a higher caliber into the teaching profession.

A few cautions are in order. We do not hold out all these programs as "exemplary." Although some are comprehensive models, others are included because a particular element or two has interest in the context of this report. In a few instances, the reforms or developments described are only now being undertaken; their promise rather than any demonstrated success recommends them. Finally, we have included several programs that offer a teacher education major; these, however, are happy examples of an integration with the liberal arts so thorough that conventional labels no longer have much meaning.

Although each of these programs is distinctive, they tend to draw on a common set of arrangements, approaches, and tactics. These include:
☐ negotiation with state education officials
☐ support from the top levels of the institution
☐ cross-disciplinary program planning
☐ high admission standards
☐ joint recruiting and advising by education and arts and sciences programs
☐ extensive requirements in the liberal arts

□ flexible formats for courses
□ team teaching
□ general-education courses focusing on educational issues
□ general-education and other liberal arts courses that meet foundations and other professional requirements
□ systematic attention to learning within the arts and sciences
□ coordinated scheduling of education and liberal arts classes
□ coordination of topics, assignments, and approaches within and between teacher education and the arts and sciences
□ consolidated professional education coursework that integrates theory and practice, content and methods
□ the study of education as a liberal art and of teaching as a subject for inquiry and reflection
□ involvement of classroom teachers and other practitioners in the program

Most importantly, these institutions have in common a determination to create and maintain strong, distinctive certification programs. It may be that this determination has been in shorter supply than ideas on how to proceed.

COLORADO COLLEGE

Teacher education has been embedded in the liberal arts for about twenty-five years at Colorado College, a private college with two thousand students in Colorado Springs. It is regarded as a campuswide commitment.

Students do not major in education; instead, prospective teachers major in a discipline within the arts and sciences. They take the same liberal arts courses and earn the same bachelor of arts degree as everyone else. By integrating study in education with the arts and sciences, the college develops teachers with the habits of mind—inquiry and critical analysis—that characterize a liberally educated individual.

Many of the subjects required for teacher certification—"History of American Education," "Education in the West," "Philosophy of Education," "Human Development," and art and music teaching, for example—are taught by faculty members from the relevant liberal arts departments. The courses are infused with content and approaches drawn from disciplines such as history, philosophy, psychology, and sociology rather than being dominated by education theory, says Charlotte Mendoza, chair of the education department.

Furthermore, the courses are shorn of redundancy to the maximum possible extent. For example, there is no "Introduction to Education" course, because, Mendoza says, "the students can learn all the concepts traditionally offered in such a course in the context of other topics." Typically, about half the students in classes that meet certification requirements are planning careers as teachers.

Citing a phrase used in the AAC survey, Mendoza states, "Our education courses 'deal with fundamental issues and reflect a breadth of intellectual concern and reference' as much as (and sometimes more than) other offerings at the college. Indeed, some of our graduates indicate that their education courses contributed the most to their 'liberal education.'"

Selection of students for the teacher education program is a multifaceted process. It begins with state requirements: all candidates for certification must pass a basic literacy test at the seventy-fifth percentile, as well as a speech test. Beyond that are Colorado College's rules: Candidates must obtain the recommendation of the chair or advisor of their major department. "Do they grasp the content sufficiently to be able to teach it?" Mendoza asks. "We don't want a poor student going out to teach."

Colorado College students who wish to be accepted into the teacher education program must volunteer in the public schools on a cocurricular basis for at least thirty hours per semester for two semesters. Serving as teacher aides, they can work with gifted or learning-disabled pupils and youngsters from disadvantaged as well as financially stable families. Based on their experience as aides, they write papers on topics such as discipline in the classroom or successful teaching strategies. They meet regularly with other aides and the elementary or secondary school coordinator to discuss their observations and experiences. The recommendation of their supervising teacher is also required for admission into the teacher education program.

The field experience serves as a screening device, Mendoza says; about 10 percent drop out after facing real youngsters in a real classroom situation. Before Mendoza instituted this admissions procedure in 1973, she says, the attrition rate in the beginning course for certification students was up to one-third. Now, she says, the attrition rate at a comparable stage is practically nil.

Candidates who remain after serving as aides write an essay explaining why they wish to become teachers.

The essay and all other information about their potential as teachers is drawn into a file examined by a panel of three interviewers: a classroom teacher, the faculty member who is a supervisor, and an education department faculty member. In the interview, candidates are judged on their ability to communicate as well as their organizational thinking, enthusiasm, motivation, and realism about their career choice.

"The college catalogue warns in bold letters, 'Admission to Colorado College does not guarantee admission to the teacher-education program,'" Mendoza points out. "I think teaching is a privilege, not a right. This is the only department in the college that can turn students away at the front door, before they've even had a chance to fail a class."

Since liberal arts faculty members handle most of the teacher preparation courses, the education department remains small, with only two full-time faculty members. Both teach occasional courses in which the majority of students are not certification candidates, as well as professional education courses. Mendoza and an English professor recently co-taught a course on "The Idea of a Liberal Education," examining a variety of ideas about what constitutes an educated person beginning with Plato's *Republic*. Most of those who took the course were first-year students whose first exposure to education theory thus took place within a liberal arts context.

Mendoza now teaches "Contemporary Educational Issues," a course that typically attracts first-year students and is not required for certification. Last year two-thirds of the students in this heavily enrolled course said at the outset that they were seriously considering teaching careers, and after studying the topic and visiting a local school most of them solidified their decision. Another course that has served to recruit students from fields such as political science, languages, and anthropology is "Dimensions of Multicultural Education," offered through the Associated Colleges of the Midwest [see ACM program description, below].

The state of Colorado has encouraged innovative programs by writing its standards not in terms of courses or semester hours but in terms of general competencies. For example, the state requires all people preparing to teach to know how to work effectively with the exceptional child. At Colorado College, no separate course is offered; the necessary theory and skills are imparted in other education courses. In "Teaching Reading in the Elementary Grades," for example, Mendoza says, "We spend some time on the slow learner. We ask, 'How will you recognize dyslexia? What could you do that would differentiate instruction for these pupils?' We focus on gifted children, too, and the students might be working with gifted children in the classroom while taking this course."

The unusual "block" system at Colorado College is conducive to fieldwork. Instead of conventional semesters or quarters in which students take a variety of courses, Colorado College divides the academic calendar into three-and-a-half week blocks, in each of which students take a single course of their choice. Since they all spend part of each day working independently, teacher aides or student teachers can conveniently spend that time in nearby classrooms.

All students at the college have the option of declaring a minor or simply taking distribution requirements; although there is no education major, there is a minor in Education Studies for those planning to teach. The difference in program may be only a few courses. The education minor can be adapted for students interested in other careers.

The administration and faculty demonstrate their respect for undergraduates who wish to pursue a teaching career in many ways. President Gresham Riley wrote in a recent college bulletin that since preparation of teachers is "a serious investigation into the nature of learning itself...we must encourage our best educated young people to enter the teaching profession. We need to impress upon them that there is no worthier calling, no better way for them to use their liberal arts education." It is the advice of faculty members in the arts and sciences departments that first prompts some of the top students to consider careers in teaching, Mendoza says. A high proportion of students in the education program graduate with honors.

With about sixty students involved in the education program and about thirteen of the 460 graduating seniors in 1986 receiving certification to teach, Mendoza acknowledges that the program is much smaller now than it was in the early 1970s, when about one-quarter of the graduating class was certified. She observes, however, "our program is better now; it's more complex, more challenging, and more selective. We attract fewer but better students. Perhaps, then, our impact can be qualitative on the teaching profession itself."

For more information, contact Charlotte Mendoza, Chair, Department of Education, Colorado College, Colorado Springs, Colo. 80903.

Washington University integrates
study of the liberal arts
with teacher preparation
by presenting education
as one of the liberal arts

WASHINGTON
UNIVERSITY

Washington University in St. Louis,
Missouri, integrates study of the liberal arts with teacher preparation by
presenting education as one of the
liberal arts. In the elementary teacher education program, practical issues of classroom teaching and
theoretical questions of purpose and
method are studied in the light of
disciplines such as psychology, sociology, and history.

Experience in schools is used to illustrate both important ideas in liberal studies and basic educational
issues. For instance, in "Educational
Psychology," which involves five
hours of classroom observation,
classroom control is examined as an
example of creating a viable social
system. In "Sociology of Education,"
day-to-day teaching decisions are
viewed in the context of the school
as a political organization, subject to
the community's values, cultures,
and economic forces.

The fact that this private university's department of education is located within its College of Arts and
Sciences is significant, says Alan
Tom, former department chair. "All
our undergraduates are liberal arts
students," he says. "The distinction
between education students and liberal arts students doesn't exist here."

The major goal of the elementary
program is to develop "reflective
practitioners." Marilyn Cohn, director of teacher education, and Tom
have written, "Teaching is a complex
intellectual activity which requires
individuals to have a knowledge of
the liberal arts, the content to be
taught, and pedagogy." It also is "a
demanding craft which entails making and carrying out an infinite
number of practical on-the-spot decisions." The reflective practitioner is
the teacher "who can confront the
realities of classroom life in a
thoughtful and knowledgeable man-
ner and can generate alternative
ways of acting."

One major strategy for developing
reflective teachers involves the integration of professional education
courses. During a "professional semester," seniors take a number of
their education courses simultaneously: "Reading Methods,"
"Mathematics Methods," "Children's
Literature," and "Principles of Teaching." Readings and assignments in
these courses are carefully coordinated. "If students took the first
three courses separately, they might
discover some of the connections on
their own," says Cohn, "but the
principles course ties them all to-

gether." Issues such as lesson planning and unit planning, classroom management and control, questioning strategies, and problem solving are raised in "Principles of Teaching," with the content of the other three courses used as examples. For instance, in the principles course students practice lesson planning by writing lessons for reading instruction. Through this internal integration, students are better able to see links among subjects.

A second strategy for developing reflective practitioners entails integration of coursework and fieldwork. Along with the principles and methods courses, students are engaged in teaching. They spend four days a week in the classrooms of nearby school districts and meet on the university campus on Fridays for their coursework. The same faculty members who teach the courses supervise the student teaching. This arrangement enables the faculty to relate concepts and strategies discussed in coursework to each student teacher's classroom setting and to encourage student reflection on these connections.

These two types of integration enable faculty members to reduce the number of separate courses in education. Students therefore can take more liberal arts courses, a third strategy for enhancing reflection on the part of elementary teacher edu-

cation students. In addition, a liberal arts orientation is characteristic of educational foundations courses such as "Sociology of Education," "Educational Psychology," and "History of Education." In fact, most students in the foundations courses are not seeking teacher certification; many of the foundations courses fulfill general education requirements for students in the College of Arts and Sciences.

As a fourth strategy for fostering reflection, the Washington University program clusters student teachers in a small number of nearby schools so that supervisors can meet regularly with cooperating teachers. In addition to consulting about the student teachers' progress, faculty members and classroom teachers can collaborate on assigned readings and the scheduling of university assignments. Clustering of student teachers also enables the students to observe and assess each other's classes, developing their skills in analysis of instruction.

The centrality of the liberal arts in the preparation of teachers is evident in the university's requirements. Students preparing to teach elementary school must take seventy-five of the 120 credits required for graduation in the arts and sciences, excluding education. Elementary education majors are urged to take a second major, or at least a minor in fields such as history, English, or one of the sci-

At the University of Dayton
the timing of specific topics
in disparate disciplines is coordinated
so students can view them
from complementary perspectives

ences. A broad base in such disciplines, they are reminded, not only enhances their teaching but enriches their intellectual lives outside the classroom.

For more information, contact Marilyn Cohn, Director of Teacher Education, Campus Box 1183, Washington University, St. Louis, Mo. 63130.

UNIVERSITY
OF DAYTON

The integration of liberal arts and professional education courses at the University of Dayton has reached the point where the timing of specific topics in disparate disciplines is coordinated so that students can view them from complementary perspectives. At the same point in the semester, for example, when students take up the events of 1789 in a course on "History of Civilization" they also examine the impact of the revolutionary period on educational theory and practice in their course on "History of Education." When epistemology is under consideration in a philosophy course offered through the arts and sciences college, the education school's course, "Growth and Development," turns

to a study of Jean Piaget's epistemological theory.

This is possible at Dayton, a Catholic institution with sixty-five hundred undergraduates in Dayton, Ohio, in part because its College of Arts and Sciences is working to coordinate courses to achieve greater coherence within its curriculum. "Our arts and sciences faculty holds three-day workshops each summer to swap syllabi, talk about themes, and alter and direct the content of courses to delineate those themes," says former arts and sciences dean Francis Lazarus. Courses then are scheduled so there is overlap and reinforcement from one discipline to another.

Dayton's integrated general education courses, for example, "deal with the phenomenon of education as a humanizing force in culture," Lazarus notes, adding, "The meaning in these subjects arises out of seeing the interrelationships." Education faculty members believe that Dayton graduates will be better equipped to construct the intellectual bridges between disciplines for their pupils, having been taught this way themselves.

A parallel effort has been undertaken at Dayton to coordinate offerings in the arts and sciences with those in education. Lazarus and teacher educators at Dayton agree that "the content of education courses, understood conceptually, and the content of arts and sciences courses are not that dissimilar."

"Such curriculum planning cannot be done casually," says Ellis Joseph, dean of the School of Education. The articulation of arts and sciences and education coursework at Dayton is the product of a four-year effort, aided by $500,000 from the National Endowment for the Humanities. As part of this process, eight members of the education faculty recently met for an entire summer term with thirteen arts and sciences faculty members. The university is contributing $25,000 in support of an additional summer workshop. Says Joseph, "You really need to support the faculty to get this kind of design."

Joseph says that Dayton's approach helps attract a greater number of liberal arts students into the field of teaching and that these students are of higher quality than recruits of the past. Several other factors have encouraged this trend at Dayton over the past two decades. Selection criteria are rigorous and standards for students in the education programs are higher than for most other majors. Students are required to maintain a higher grade point average and to complete three hundred hours of fieldwork by the end of their junior year. Education students also must take more liberal arts courses than professional courses,

though the line between the two categories is blurring to some extent as the courses are increasingly integrated.

Recruitment of new students is another area of cooperation between the liberal arts and education faculties at Dayton. Every spring and fall a joint orientation session is held for high school seniors; even the brochure is a joint effort. "We give them an orientation on what it means to study to become a teacher," Joseph says. "We introduce them to the subjects they would study, pointing out the courses they will need in order to become well-educated teachers." The visitors attend simulated classes as well as regular classes in the education school. Students who wish to major in arts and sciences and are interested in certification are advised at these recruiting sessions and, when enrolled, by both faculties. The sessions typically are attended by twenty-five to fifty high school seniors; about 80 percent of those attending decide to enter Dayton.

A course in philosophy of education serves as the capstone for Dayton students. "We not only discuss idealism, pragmatism, and all the other 'isms,' " Joseph says, "but also conduct a dialogue about what schools are for. Some think schools ought to prepare kids for a vocation. Some think they should prepare people for college. Some feel there is

Integration of the liberal arts
with professional preparation at Princeton
...means finding the relevance
of education in each
of the liberal arts disciplines

one curriculum that is good for everyone for all time. We want to familiarize them with what the American debate on these questions has been. Some day, when these students assume positions of leadership in the community and in teaching, they can make their voices heard."

For more information, contact Ellis Joseph, Dean, School of Education, University of Dayton, 300 College Park, Dayton, Ohio 45469.

PRINCETON
UNIVERSITY

When the Princeton University faculty decided twenty years ago, at the request of undergraduates, to offer a program to prepare secondary school teachers, they already had in place nearly all the courses they would need in the core liberal arts curriculum. Princeton recognized that "a number of existing courses were, in fact, foundations courses for teachers," says Henry N. Drewry, director of the Teacher Preparation Program (TPP), "and they also happened to be solid liberal arts courses." Integration of the liberal arts with professional preparation at this private, selective university with forty-four hundred

undergraduates means finding the relevance of education in each of the liberal arts disciplines.

For example, "Philosophical Foundations of Democracy" does not deal exclusively with education, Henry says, "but you can't effectively talk about the bases on which the American system was founded without discussing education. Education, in fact, always has been included as an important part of what the faculty member addressed." Although the course covers several topics in addition to education, it does fulfill a New Jersey state certification requirement in the foundations area.

A course offered in the sociology department entitled "Social and Cultural Aspects of Education" deals with education as a major socializing institution in American life; public schooling obviously is central to such a topic, and this course also meets a foundations requirement for education. "Educational Psychology," "History of Education," and "Philosophy of the Behavioral Sciences" are other courses that meet state requirements but were offered to undergraduates before the faculty decided to establish a program for the preparation of teachers.

"Without our consciously thinking about teaching, the liberal arts curriculum has done what I think it should do," says Drewry. "It has included a number of courses relevant to teachers and vital to anyone seeking a solid liberal arts background as well. It wasn't that the faculty moved away from traditional content to deal with education in these courses. They appropriately included education as an important part of their subject."

Two additional experiences were added to the regular undergraduate curriculum to meet New Jersey state standards for secondary teacher certification: a seminar on general teaching methods and full-time practice teaching experience in the public schools. The two occur together in one semester of the senior year.

Since the eight-week senior year practicum gives students their chief opportunity to acquire experience teaching their subject, the cooperating teachers who supervise them in the classroom are screened and selected with special care and with the aid of school administrators. Cooperating teachers must be expert not only at classroom teaching but also at elucidating in a tutorial setting what constitutes successful teaching. Training sessions are held at Princeton every year for the pool of thirty to thirty-five cooperating teachers. Those who consent to supervise and tutor seniors are appointed by the dean of the faculty as consultants to TPP. They receive a stipend and access to Princeton facilities, including the library, for a full year.

Even with students as bright as Princeton undergraduates, Drewry says, and even with the thirteen-week general methods seminar taught by two outstanding and experienced classroom instructors, the main problem is the same as in all teacher training—"coming to recognize how one translates what one has learned into methods to help others learn it." One of the chief ways TPP addresses this is through close contact with each of the students in the program. "We have a small program; we try for fifteen seniors a year," Drewry explains. "We invite freshmen and sophomores to come talk with us, and by their junior year, when they are officially in the program, we've gotten to know them reasonably well. We work at establishing a collegial relationship that makes it possible to say things to each other and be heard."

Drewry and other Princeton faculty members often suggest to the prospective teachers that they reach back in their memories to recall techniques used by effective teachers they have encountered in their own schooling. Just as often, Drewry says, they remind students of relevant information encountered in their liberal arts courses at the university and help them see how that information can apply to a specific pedagogical question. By drawing students' attention to the many ways in which the liberal arts serve teaching, Princeton faculty members reinforce the idea of mutual dependency between education and the liberal arts.

Faculty members from sociology, English, political science, romance languages, and geology serve with Drewry, a history professor, on a TPP Interdepartmental Committee to set policy for the program. "Each of them is deeply concerned about the quality of the education students have had before they reach us here," Drewry says, and they are among the faculty members who guide undergraduates preparing to teach. Informal contacts thus supplement formal instruction to promote the students' exploration of teaching theory and methodology.

The cooperation of state officials has helped Princeton play a role in efforts to attract excellent students into teaching careers, says Drewry, but state approval of TPP was not as hard to come by as many expected. "There wasn't a great debate about these things, no big difference of opinion," says Drewry, who has been TPP director since the program's inception. "State officials have given us good support and encouragement, making it possible for people who have not taken the traditional 'education approach' to be successful as teachers." He stresses, however, that the state does not give Princeton any special assistance. "One has to have

a good rationale, and it has to fit criteria set in the standards."

For example, a state requirement for future teachers to study reading methods is met within "Psychology of Education." One of the precepts—a small discussion section led by a faculty member—devotes a block of time to the topic. In addition, a noncredit course taught by a reading specialist in local schools—an extremely good teacher, Drewry says—is required by TPP and usually is taken in the sophomore year.

A few features of the program have been challenged by state education officials, but in each case Drewry says the state officials were willing to negotiate a solution. For example, a full semester of practice teaching usually is required, but the state will accept an eight-week period for students who, in the process of their entire preparation, complete fieldwork—including classroom observation, tutoring, and other structured activities with elementary or secondary youngsters—equal to a full semester. The TPP office helps place students as tutors in their ongoing community program, as teaching assistants in the summer middle-school program offered at Princeton, and in similar settings. "Most students who have an interest in teaching are getting into these kinds of activities anyway," he says, noting that fieldwork experiences are documented to be sure they meet state standards.

Recently the state decided that practice teachers must be supervised by individuals with expertise in the subject area. Until recently, the program has relied for supervision on a specially recruited group of experienced classroom teachers working out of the TPP office, as well as on the cooperating teachers, and only occasional visits by faculty members. Drewry says that this new concern will be accommodated by increasing the number of visits from Princeton faculty members in the practice teacher's field.

TPP assumes responsibility for making sure that required courses provide the content identified in the state standards. "Our liberal arts courses change from time to time," says Drewry, noting that they often defy neat description in a brochure. "A faculty member offers a course once a year. If that faculty member is away—which is not unusual—the course may change, even though it has the same name." It is sometimes the students who call a course's shortcomings to the attention of TPP, he says.

In Drewry's view, Princeton's approach to teacher preparation could be adopted by other institutions, including those with less selective admissions. He acknowledges that size is a crucial factor; because of the need for top-notch cooperating

teachers, it would be difficult for Princeton to continue TPP in its present format if the number of participants were some multiple of what it is now. He notes, however, that as current efforts by school districts to upgrade the quality of teaching prove fruitful, this would be less of an obstacle.

A creative look at existing courses to spotlight the content essential for teachers could prove advantageous even at larger institutions, Drewry believes. "It seems to me there is a natural relationship between what any good course has to say and a course about how one prepares to teach," he says. "If there is a problem in what is identified as education courses in some places, it may be because they limit themselves too much."

For more information, contact Henry Drewry, Director, Teacher Preparation Program, Princeton University, Princeton, N.J. 08544.

ALVERNO COLLEGE

Attending Alverno College and preparing for a teaching career means trying constantly to define the meaning of a liberal education. The college experience has been thoroughly restructured since 1970 to place priority on the abilities the students will acquire rather than the knowledge the faculty has to impart. As a result, although only four hundred of the two thousand undergraduates at this private college for women in Milwaukee, Wisconsin, are preparing for teaching careers, every undergraduate is continuously made conscious of issues relating to curriculum development, learning theory, and proficiency assessment; from her arrival onward, each is encouraged to reflect on her experiences and translate the ethos of a liberal education into personal terms.

The curriculum has been designed to develop skills and abilities that the faculty considers essential for any college graduate. These "outcomes" are effective communication, analysis, problem-solving, social interaction, responsibility for global environment, effective citizenship, and aesthetic responsiveness. For each outcome the faculty has defined four sequential levels of mastery that all undergraduates must demonstrate, and another two levels that students must demonstrate in the context of their major fields.

Education majors must demonstrate five skills before graduating: conceptualization, diagnosis, coordination, communication, and inte-

grative interaction. Each of these is carefully defined in writing so that all faculty members and students understand the criteria by which students will be assessed. "Communication" in the context of teacher preparation therefore includes not only the abilities required of all Alverno students—reading, writing, listening, speaking, quantitative literacy, and computer literacy—but also the ability to give clear presentations, set goals, give and receive feedback, and convey enthusiasm.

The student outcomes inculcated by the curriculum, integrating both active and reflective qualities in the learner, are developed and assessed in the context of all Alverno courses. Assessments—Alverno's version of tests—start with simple performances. For example, a beginning student demonstrates that she can distinguish between "observations" and "inferences" as part of her analytical ability in the context of an English lesson, a psychology class, or a science course. By the third or fourth year of college, assessments involve complex integration of several of the essential outcomes, drawing on information acquired in diverse courses. Students are encouraged in every class to bring up information and use abilities developed in other classes.

Professor Mary Diez, education division chair, acknowledges that the curricular focus on integrating knowledge and abilities can be daunting at first for both new students and new faculty members. She and her colleagues are convinced, however, that the long-term benefits are well worth the effort. For undergraduates who hope to become teachers, the process is particularly useful, she points out, since they are continually viewing their coursework from the perspective of how to acquire the abilities fundamental to a liberal education. "The students absorb from the general atmosphere reflective habits of thought that can enhance their experiences for the rest of their lives," she says. "They gain specific skills in self-assessment and get pretty articulate about what they know and what they can do."

Future teachers at Alverno take the same general-education core as the rest of the students. All majors build on the abilities developed in the liberal arts courses required in the first four semesters of the curriculum; it is only in the advanced-level work in the last four semesters that the differentiation between majors becomes clear.

Alverno's environment fosters self-consciousness about liberal learning, thus encouraging many students to consider seriously the possibility of teaching as a profession. Diez says that Alverno's pervasive attention to the education process instills future

teachers on campus with pride in their profession. "They have a sense of self-esteem, and that encourages their being more critical of their classes," she says. At its best, she maintains, this environment produces not only liberally educated teachers but teachers who are unusually cognizant of what it takes to make others liberally educated.

For more information, contact Mary Diez, Chair, Education Division, Alverno College, 3401 South 39th Street, Milwaukee, Wis. 53215-4020.

ST. NORBERT'S COLLEGE

St. Norbert's College, a private institution in DePere, Wisconsin, with seventeen hundred undergraduates, approaches scheduling in a way that enables undergraduates to complete a teacher certification program with a hefty liberal arts component within four years. The program, in place for ten years, features—long before the final year of college—classroom teaching experience concurrent with education coursework and an extensive use of general-education courses to meet professional education requirements.

Offering students practical experience
as well as academic study of education
early in their college careers
is a critical part of the program
at St. Norbert's College

Under the "sophomore block" system, students interested in a teaching career set aside the spring semester of their second year to concentrate on education courses. For ten of the fifteen weeks of the semester, they take five of the courses required for certification. They spend the remaining five weeks in the local schools full time as "pre-student teachers," becoming acquainted with the elementary or secondary classroom from the perspective of a professional educator.

The courses taken concurrently in the block for secondary majors are "Foundations," which may emphasize history, philosophy, or sociology; "Psychology of Learning"; "Classroom Evaluation"; "Technology of Education," involving computer use; and "Exceptional Children."

There are both pragmatic and philosophical reasons for the system, says E. Thomas de Wane, director of teacher education. The philosophical reasons relate, he says, to "raising the consciousness level of our students" early in their studies. "Their clinical experience helps them subsequently to discern dimensions of knowledge that apply to them as teachers. When they proceed to take other liberal arts courses, they can adapt much of what they learn to their role as teachers. They can view what they learn within the context of how they learn it."

Offering students practical experience as well as academic study of education early in their college careers is a critical part of the program. The amount of actual teaching St. Norbert's sophomores do varies, but the cooperating teachers are asked to let them conduct at least a three-day unit or its equivalent.

Among the pragmatic reasons for offering students early clinical experience is the ability to complete certification requirements within four years—a highly desirable goal, in de Wane's view. "We give the students the background they need for teaching," he says, "but then let them go out and learn it experientially. To prolong the coursework would not be acceptable."

For someone who wants secondary school certification, the sophomore block provides all education courses required before student teaching except one—"Methods in Reading" in the chosen subject, which can be taken subsequently. During the semester in which students practice-teach, they also study general methods and methods in a content area. Students aiming at elementary accreditation have more requirements in the education department, but a substantial core can be completed during the sophomore block.

An important advantage of the sophomore block is that it provides a chance for the supervising faculty member and cooperating teacher to identify and remedy, at an early stage, problems the student may encounter in teaching. It helps students determine whether they are suited for teaching at a point when there is still time to pursue other options. About sixty students enroll in the program each year, typically twice as many in elementary as in secondary certification programs, de Wane says. Nearly all of them choose to become teachers. He estimates that only about 5 percent of those who wish to continue are advised not to do so.

Scheduling of the sophomore block is relatively easy at St. Norbert's because the fundamental record keeping unit is the course, not the credit. Several education courses are logged as "half-courses"; the clinical experience also counts as a half-course. The six "half-courses" offered during the sophomore block therefore are reckoned as three courses.

Students who wish to take an additional course during that semester—secondary certificate candidates who want a course in their major field, for example—may do so. Since other courses in the college run the full semester, and since the student is off campus for much of the final five weeks, any additional course has to be scheduled either early in the morning or late in the afternoon. Arts and sciences faculty members cooperate by scheduling appropriate classes at these hours.

The chief drawback of the system—and at the same time, de Wane says, a key strength—is the intensity of the sophomore block semester. The "half-courses" actually are two-thirds courses, since they run ten out of fifteen weeks and, like all St. Norbert's courses, involve four hours of class per week. "It does cram a lot of academic work into ten weeks," he says. "Students find themselves quite burdened, to be honest." The college does what it can to offset the pressure; for instance, education faculty members try to stagger tests and term paper assignments.

This very intensity is worthwhile, St. Norbert educators believe, since studying so many fundamentals of education concurrently enables prospective teachers to perceive connections within the material that might otherwise be harder to see. It also reinforces the student's understanding that teacher preparation, like teaching, is an intellectually rigorous endeavor.

Finally—and this is the key to St. Norbert's ability to offer a four-year program—all relevant general-education offerings are used to meet professional requirements. The education department specifies eleven of the twelve general-education distribution requirements for its majors. For instance, St. Norbert's students choose between courses on Greek

Eastern Michigan University's teacher education program in science combines academic rigor with awareness of how to teach what one is learning

philosophy and the philosophy of human nature; teacher education students must take the latter to fulfill their requirement. The sociology course "Race and Ethnicity," to use another example, fulfills the requirement for multicultural competency.

In some cases, general-education courses fulfill part of a given certification requirement, and the rest is met by one or more other courses. For instance, "Race and Ethnicity" partially fulfills the human relations requirement, and the remainder is met by a course in philosophy of religion. These kinds of arrangements save time in students' programs. They also emphasize for them the relevance to teaching of their study in the liberal arts.

For more information, contact E. Thomas de Wane, Director, Teacher Education, Saint Norbert College, De Pere, Wis. 54115.

EASTERN
MICHIGAN
UNIVERSITY

Elementary school teachers supervising student teachers from Eastern Michigan University in Ypsilanti frequently ask the undergraduates to handle the entire science unit from the outset, and the EMU students are able and eager to oblige. The reason for the classroom teachers' unusual confidence in the student teachers' ability to teach science is an EMU program that exemplifies how liberal arts can successfully be blended with professional preparation.

EMU's Preservice Elementary Teacher Education Program in Science combines academic rigor in science disciplines with awareness of how to teach what one is learning. It is a four-course sequence that emphasizes the connections among all the science disciplines, such as standard methods of scientific inquiry, so that the future teachers can help their pupils see those links as well. Instead of appearing in a separate methods course, methodology is incorporated into courses on physics, chemistry, earth sciences (geology and geography), and biology offered by the respective departments within the College of Arts and Sciences. The instructors—all arts and sciences faculty members—introduce teaching methods as they are appropriate, "striking while the iron is hot," says chemistry professor Donald B. Phillips.

Chemistry laboratory experiments in the EMU preservice program illustrate how college-level learning combines with strategies for elementary-level teaching. Half the activities involved in these experiments are like those offered in any college lab, testing theoretical hypotheses at a sophisticated level. The other half demonstrate aspects of those principles that elementary school pupils can grasp. Materials that are readily available in a grocery store or drugstore are used so that student teachers can easily design parallel experiments for their pupils. For instance, Phillips says, paper chromatography lends itself to dramatic illustration through the use of no more than coffee-filter paper, water-soluble marking pens, and a peanut butter jar. He says that his EMU students gain a more solid understanding of theory by reconsidering it from the perspective of the elementary pupil. Indeed, he believes, the task of devising ways to convey scientific principles to youngsters in itself effectively reinforces the students' learning of the material.

The science faculty members who teach the preservice courses all have had experience in public school teaching and/or in teacher education; their strong teaching background is one of the advantages EMU enjoys as a former normal school, says W. Scott Westerman, dean of the College of Education.

The state of Michigan has a tradition, predating the current nationwide debate by at least forty years, of not sanctioning the offering of majors in education except in special cases; by law, the only undergraduate education majors are those seeking certification in special education, physical education, and vocational subjects. Otherwise, prospective teachers pursue discipline-based majors in the arts and sciences. Last year EMU recommended about 270 B.A. recipients for elementary certification and 130 for secondary.

The preservice program is the result of collaboration among EMU's four science faculties and its College of Education. It was instituted as a pilot program in 1969 and became a requirement for certification in elementary science teaching six years later. Its success is reflected in the increase in the numbers of students choosing teaching careers in math and the natural sciences, Westerman says. Last year there were 152 math majors seeking secondary certification, four times more than there were five years before. There also were eight physics majors at EMU who planned to teach. Although this number is small, three years before there were four in the entire state.

Teacher educators at EMU have made special efforts to recruit math and science majors for teacher certification programs. Last year, they sent letters to the homes of one thousand undergraduates who were majoring in math or science. They sent the letters at Thanksgiving,

The fourteen small liberal arts colleges that constitute the Associated Colleges of the Midwest share...an off-campus urban study program

when students could more readily discuss with their parents the possibilities of planning for a teaching career. The letters invited interested students to an informational meeting. One hundred attended, Westerman says, and a significant number of them ultimately enrolled.

Westerman chairs a university-wide council on teacher education that coordinates teacher education programs at EMU and last year completed a major revamping of the entire teacher education curriculum. A majority of the seventeen council members are from liberal arts disciplines outside the education college. "There isn't that big a moat to be bridged here between the arts and sciences faculties and the College of Education," he says. By integrating the basic sciences and incorporating teaching methods into the framework of the subject matter, the pre-service science teaching program demonstrates the benefits that can come from collaboration.

For more information, contact W. Scott Westerman, Dean of Education, Eastern Michigan University, Ypsilanti, Mich. 48197.

ASSOCIATED COLLEGES OF THE MIDWEST

Education reform at the state and national levels can pose special problems for small institutions. Administrators and faculty members may see the goals of new requirements in teacher education as worthy but may lack the means to implement them. One example is a requirement aimed at strengthening future teachers' backgrounds in multicultural experiences and understanding. How can a small college afford not only the time but also the faculty to provide meaningful coverage of such a topic? Moreover, if a campus is located in a rural or isolated area, how can it offer student teachers experiential access to the cultural diversity that will broaden their perspectives and enhance their ability to teach in an increasingly multicultural world?

One answer is suggested by the Associated Colleges of the Midwest (ACM), a consortium formed thirty years ago to pool resources for programs that are beyond the means of its individual members. The fourteen small liberal arts colleges that now constitute ACM share fourteen nationally and internationally based off-campus study programs—including the Urban Education Program (UEP) in Chicago, the only program among the fourteen with a focus on the topic of education. UEP offers students from all the member campuses a chance to work in Chicago metropolitan-area schools with classroom populations so culturally and linguistically varied that they often are characterized as microcosms of the world.

The colleges in the consortium—each with a student body of fewer than thirty-five hundred students and almost all located far from any metropolitan center—are Beloit, Carleton, Colorado, Coe, Cornell, Grinnell, Knox, Lake Forest, Macalester, Monmouth, Ripon, St. Olaf, and the College of the University of Chicago. UEP represents an affirmation of these institutions' belief in the importance of education as an area of study within the undergraduate liberal education program. As with all ACM programs, UEP is open to any qualified student from a member campus as well as to a limited number of students from selected Great Lakes Colleges Association institutions, depending on available space.

UEP has three basic options in which students can participate: a month-long intensive course entitled "Dimensions of Multicultural and Global Awareness," a semester or term of student teaching in urban schools, and accredited programs in bilingual teacher training and teaching English as a second language (TESL). All of these options introduce students to issues in urban education in ways that enhance their liberal education.

The "Dimensions" course has as its primary goal the deepening of students' theoretical and experiential understanding of multicultural and global issues. The month-long intensive course is offered three times yearly to fit into the interim periods between college semesters. Typically about fifty first- and second-year students participate, since this is considered an introductory course with a broad range of possible exploratory field experiences.

The schedule divides each day into three segments. The morning is for field experience. Students can choose to work in one school as a teacher-assistant for the entire month. Placements for this option are at either multiethnic/multilingual schools or schools serving a specific cultural/linguistic group. As a second option, students can elect to work on an international team (consisting of international and American students) developing presentations about a particular region of the world or cross-cultural topic (for example, law, religion, or culture). In this case, the team ultimately makes several presentations to as many as five hundred students in two to seven different schools, all within a period of one month. In either case, student projects focus on teaching and learning about different world populations and world issues.

In the afternoons, students meet with UEP staff members and/or guest speakers for a series of seminars based on the skills outlined by Robert Hanvey in his monograph, *An Attainable Global Perspective*. Starting with their own concepts of geography and history, students examine their own perspectives and begin to look at and listen to the viewpoints and realities of people with diverse cultural backgrounds. The course emphasizes "how to use diversity as an asset rather than a liability in the educational process," says UEP director Marilyn Turkovich.

Simply by living in Chicago, students can confront a spectrum of cultures broader than that afforded by any small town. The program's evening and weekend activities take advantage of this fact. Numerous field trips are arranged into the neighborhood communities of Chicago. Students are encouraged to participate in as many trips as they can throughout the month, and most students do everything scheduled. Experiences provided regularly are walking tours of neighborhoods (Polish, south Asian, Indian, Mexican, Puerto Rican, Vietnamese, and

others), conversations and discussions with community leaders and residents, and a day-long bus tour of the city led by a local urbanologist who traces immigration patterns in Chicago since the mid-nineteenth century.

About half of the one hundred students who participate in UEP in an average year are enrolled in the Dimensions course; the other half are student teachers. Student teaching in UEP is a full-time commitment and lasts from twelve to sixteen weeks, depending on the home campus calendar. Placements are made at any grade level in public or private schools, according to the specific needs of the students. Requests for special placements such as Montessori, special education, juvenile detention centers, or arts-education institutions also can be honored due to the vast resources of the city.

UEP has a full-time staff of five persons administering and teaching the program in Chicago. The staff stays in close contact with education faculty members at all participating colleges, visiting the campuses twice yearly. "We're an extension of each of those departments," says Turkovich. UEP also brings together the education faculties of the participating schools at least once a year, Turkovich says, "to learn from each other and generate new directions for program development." The UEP staff works closely with liberal arts faculty members at all the campuses to encourage integration of all areas of study into the education programs at each institution.

Participation in the program often results in a student's returning to Chicago in one way or another, either to study more or to work in the schools. The "Dimensions" and introductory TESL courses attract students who are considering teaching as a profession as well as students interested in other fields. Turkovich says it is not uncommon, however, for students who were undecided about their careers—or who were certain they did not want to teach—to be drawn into teaching by their experience in these intensive courses. Four such students from among the thirty-nine enrolled in the Dimensions course last January "were fascinated by the Chicago teaching experience," Turkovich says, and subsequently applied for admission to education departments on their respective campuses.

For more information, contact Marilyn Turkovich, Director, Urban Education Program, Associated Colleges of the Midwest, 5633 North Kenmore, Chicago, Ill. 60660.

WESLEYAN UNIVERSITY

A course that combines readings from Plato, Montaigne, Whitehead, and Dewey with techniques of lesson plan preparation, classroom management, and learning assessment is the "watershed" course in Wesleyan University's teacher preparation program. Entitled "The Craft of Teaching," it is offered to seniors in the fall semester, just before they begin student teaching. "This course is the bridge between core theoretical courses like philosophy and psychology of education and specific courses on teaching any discipline," says Marjorie Rosenbaum, director of the Educational Studies Program (ESP) and creator of the course.

There are no education majors and no department of education at Wesleyan, a private university with twenty-seven hundred undergraduates in Middletown, Connecticut. All students major in the liberal arts. ESP offers twelve courses that are popular enough to draw up to four hundred students annually. Although only twenty-five to thirty students are recommended for certification in any one year, the rest also benefit from studying education in a liberal arts context. ESP offers certification for seventh through twelfth grade levels; students seeking elementary certification can obtain it through a consortial arrangement with St. Joseph's College in West Hartford and the Rocky Hill school district.

"The Craft of Teaching" replaced "General Methods and Principles of Teaching" in 1983, after the state of Connecticut began requiring teacher certification programs to cover three new areas: special education; abuse of drugs, alcohol, and tobacco; and intergroup relations. Rosenbaum combined all these topics into Wesleyan's basic methodology course, which not only gained state approval but has been circulated by the state to all teacher preparatory institutions as a model.

The bridging function of the course is evident in the reading list, which combines major works of social criticism, philosophy, and history with concrete handbooks of pedagogy. Strike and Soltis' *The Ethics of Teaching* and Bruner's *In Search of Mind: Essays in Autobiography* appear with Cooper's *Classroom Teaching Skills* and Morsink's *Teaching Special Needs Students in Regular Classrooms* among the required books. Postman and Weingartner's *Teaching as a Subversive Activity* and Friere's *Pedagogy of the Oppressed*

share the recommended reading list with *High School: A Report on Secondary Education*, Goodman's *Handbook on Contemporary Education*, Grambs and Carr's *Modern Methods in Secondary Education*, *Preparing Instructional Objectives*, and Schmuck's *Group Process in the Classroom*. Rosenbaum believes that integrating several disciplines and practical techniques into one course demonstrates to students how intricately all these are woven into a teacher's responsibilities on a daily basis.

The seventeen-page syllabus suggests further juxtapositions: Mortimer J. Adler is discussed on the same day that the Connecticut Standards for Teacher Preparation are distributed. Rosenbaum asserts that the connections between the basic liberal arts and practical teaching techniques must be constantly stressed. For instance, a teacher needs a thorough understanding of a novel, historical period, or scientific law to make an appropriate selection of materials, then understanding of a range of strategies and techniques to determine the most appropriate method of instruction.

"The Craft of Teaching" is a double-credit course—seven credit hours instead of the standard three-and-a-half. It helps meet teaching certification requirements as well as general education requirements for Wesleyan students.

Whether they are reading Plato or Postman, the class typically breaks into small groups to discuss a few overriding questions. In the case of Whitehead's *The Aims of Education*, for example, Rosenbaum asks students, "What are his 'rhythms of education' and why did he think they are significant? Do you think they matter in 1988?" Rosenbaum explains, "Whitehead begins with the age of romance and moves to an age of precision, then generalization. That is how you teach anyone anything. First they're in love with it, then they get good at it, then they see how it affects everything else."

As the course progresses, she says, the ideas the students have explored in their reading of great thinkers will surface again and again. When they are preparing their own lesson plans, Rosenbaum reminds them of the insights and convictions expressed in those discussions and makes sure they recognize the connections and apply them. In the "Craft" course as in ESP generally, she says, "there is nothing redundant, but there are echoes" of themes essential for teachers to master.

Rosenbaum has worked with a co-teacher each year; a public school teacher, professors of psychology and history, and, most recently, the superintendent of a local school system have shared instructional duties with her. In each case they have helped illustrate the connections between liberal arts preparation and effective teaching, Rosenbaum says. She also has invited local administrators and school board members to meet with the students, "to explain what they do and why, so future teachers can gain a sense of the interplay between people who make policy and those who carry it out. It helps to meet real people who do the real work." Wesleyan's student teachers, who are one semester ahead of the students in the course, and program alumni have addressed the class to bring home the practicalities of the job as well.

"The Craft of Teaching" emphasizes "the many faces of teaching— teacher as decision maker, presenter, inviter, facilitator of learning, and teacher as nurturer, as person," says Rosenbaum. By the time students reach the course's "closing synthesis" and submit required educational autobiographies, Rosenbaum says, they understand in personal terms a statement in another of the books they have read, Philip Rieff's *Fellow Teachers: Of Culture and Its Second Death*: "To be a scholar-teacher, neither guru nor entrepreneur, is to continue the life of study; at best, a scholar-teacher is a virtuoso student."

For more information, contact Marjorie Rosenbaum, Director, Educational Studies Program, Wesleyan University, Middletown, Conn. 06457.

HAMPSHIRE COLLEGE

In existence only since 1970, Hampshire College takes a distinctive approach to undergraduate education: one that focuses on critical inquiry. In this educational system each student, in consultation with a faculty committee, designs a worthy and coherent individualized program of study. He or she then compiles and presents a portfolio of work, including papers associated with specific courses as well as independent research, course evaluations and grades, and letters of support.

Hampshire first offered a teacher education program soon after the college's founding. In its first decade, however, the program was identified almost exclusively with certification. Conventional in approach, it was set apart from the rest of Hampshire's liberal arts curriculum.

With a grant from the Consortium for the Advancement of Private Higher Education, Hampshire College now is creating a new interdisciplinary program in education studies. This program—Hampshire offers no majors—will serve students with a wide range of interests in cul-

tural and social issues. It will embody the college's critical inquiry approach to liberal education and include a strong emphasis on multicultural education. According to Professor Frederick Weaver, who helped develop the program, it reflects the belief that the traditional liberal arts disciplines do not hold a monopoly on subject matter appropriate for liberal education. Elementary and secondary education are important topics whose complexity calls for examination from diverse perspectives. The field of education can be taught in ways that promote the development of students' critical intelligence, and its subject matter can be the basis of an exciting and rigorous liberal education.

For example, says Weaver, courses in the mechanics and methods of teaching can become lively intellectual experiences when students are encouraged to recognize the ways in which every prescription about proper lesson plan development and every experiment designed to test the efficacy of a particular teaching method embodies myriad assumptions about the subject matter or skill being taught; the nature of human cognition; the backgrounds of students; the patterns of authority in the classroom, school, and system; and the relationship between schooling and society. When taught this way, education becomes an intellectually compelling field of inquiry, and students learn to appreciate, by studying teaching and learning in a variety of contexts, the extent to which schools are key social and cultural institutions—influencing as well as reflecting the directions of American thought and life.

Hampshire College's new Education Studies Program will be organized into two curricula—one focused on child development, cognition, and the classroom and the other on schools and schooling as key social and cultural institutions. The first curriculum will be strongly influenced by cognitive science, which—with its emphasis on theoretical and empirical studies of human cognition—offers intellectually demanding and rewarding approach, in the view of program planners, than standard educational psychology. Hampshire faculty members anticipate that, while meeting requirements for certification, students who work in this curriculum will formulate concentrations around issues such as language acquisition, educational testing, environmental education, gender roles, and the place of mathematical and scientific learning in cognitive development. In all cases, Hampshire will offer students in education studies a range of complementary opportunities for experiential learning.

The second curriculum within education studies will focus on current educational issues in the United States in their historical contexts. Student concentrations will be organized around topics such as teaching as a profession (including unionization and the historical role of women teachers), the changing character of schools' missions and purposes, public policy regarding education, economics of education, debates on social mobility and the screening function of education (with particular attention to racial minorities), postsecondary education, and the role of parents in educating their children. This curriculum will draw from a wide range of social science and humanities courses.

These two education studies curricula, each with its separate field of inquiry and focus, are related as well. The principle underlying both is that broadly conceived studies of educational institutions must be informed by a solid understanding of child development and learning theory and, conversely, that studies of teaching and learning must be firmly set in more general historical and social contexts to give meaning to classroom-level studies.

The Hampshire Education Studies Program is significant because education will not be studied in separation from the liberal arts curriculum but through it. By presenting the field of education as a challenging, exciting area of inquiry, Hampshire hopes to make teacher education more attractive to talented young people and to produce the kinds of teachers who will be innovators in public education and who will contribute to the momentum of educational reform.

For more information, contact Frederick Weaver, Director, Institutional Research and Academic Planning, Hampshire College, Amherst, Mass. 01002.

UNIVERSITY OF TULSA

In 1984, the Oklahoma State Board of Education adopted a revised set of teacher certification standards that require teacher education students to take as many as seventy semester hours of professional education courses. Because these requirements threatened to make a new integrated liberal arts/teacher education program at the University of Tulsa impossible, the university sought—and eventually won—a special exemption from these regulations.

In 1984, with substantial support from the National Endowment for the Humanities, the University of Tulsa implemented the "Tulsa Curriculum." This nationally recognized general-education core curriculum, now required of all Tulsa students, focuses on the significant ideas of Western and other cultures through the study of primary texts. It is intended to introduce students to the basic areas of knowledge, including the humanities, the arts, the social sciences, and the sciences. At the same time, it attempts to teach the skills of critical thinking and writing necessary to use this knowledge effectively. The twenty-seven-hour core curriculum includes nine hours of writing (three of which are in small, interdisciplinary "First Seminars"); foreign language through the second year or, in the case of science majors, math through calculus; a capstone course called the "Senior Seminar"; and a computer literacy requirement. Additional general-education requirements call for thirty hours of coursework distributed across several curricular areas.

In June 1985, as part of its curricular reform program, the university abolished its College of Education and placed all teacher education programs in the College of Arts and Sciences. This made possible implementation of the Tulsa Teacher Education Program, a program that integrates professional study with liberal arts coursework. The key element of this program is the requirement that, in addition to the Tulsa Curriculum, all students seeking to teach must complete a double major: one consisting of thirty-four semester hours of education courses (including twelve hours of student teaching and streamlined and integrated methods and reading courses) and the other in an academic area, consisting of at least forty hours of courses. Two-thirds of the coursework in the academic major and one-half of the coursework in the education major must be at an advanced level.

Students seeking elementary certification must complete the same requirements as those seeking secondary certification except one. Instead of a forty-hour academic major, these students take a "short major" consisting of twenty-five semester hours selected by the academic department. This shorter major allows elementary education students the time to complete a special twenty-seven semester hour interdisciplinary program taught by both education and arts and sciences faculty members and focusing on the world of the child. Specifically, they complete four blocks of courses. One nine-hour block emphasizes social development, cognitive development, linguistics, and theories of socialization. The other blocks focus on communication, aesthetics, and scientific inquiry and problem solving.

The Tulsa Teacher Education Program was designed specifically to enable students to complete its challenging requirements in four years. Moreover, according to Susan Resneck Parr, Dean of Arts and Sciences, it was designed to encourage more students—particularly those in the liberal arts—to consider teaching as a possible career. Conventional teacher preparation programs that require students to decide between a concentration in teacher preparation or in a subject area tend to discourage student exploration of the education option. Because the Tulsa program allows them to do both, they can decide to choose teaching relatively late in their college career. At the same time, the program's rigorous liberal arts requirements ensure that its teacher education graduates have a solid background in content areas. A further benefit of the Tulsa program, made possible by the integration of the colleges of education and arts and sciences, is increased understanding on the part of the liberal arts faculty of teacher education and certification, and increased respect for the education faculty.

Planned program evaluations have not yet been conducted. Anecdotal evidence, however, suggests that the program will be successful. NTE scores already have improved and faculty members believe that the program is attracting higher quality students. At present, the Tulsa Program is a rigorous alternative to the general state program. Warren Hipsher, chair of the education faculty at Tulsa, believes that in the future it will be a model for educational reform throughout the state.

The existence of the Tulsa Teacher Education Program was threatened by the 1984 change in state requirements. According to Parr, those requirements, which stressed professional education, were incompatible, both in spirit and in practice, with those of the Tulsa program. Although the new state requirements were rigorous, students could meet them without studying in depth the subjects they would teach. Moreover, much of their time would be devoted to the kinds of traditional methods and readings courses that often have been criticized as repetitive and unchallenging.

It also would have been impossible to complete all the requirements of both the state program and the Tulsa program within a four-year period. Extending the program to five or five-and-a-half years to allow students to complete both, on the other hand, would not only make it too expensive but lack any plausible educational rationale. According to Parr, because the faculty and administration believed that there was no chance of changing the state requirements, they decided to seek a special exemption.

The negotiations that led to the granting of the exemption began with a series of discussions with the State Superintendent of Education, the Professional Standards Board, and other deans of education throughout the state. The Tulsa proposal initially was received coolly, according to Parr. Most of those involved in the discussions, as well as many officials of the state's teacher's union, had participated in the negotiations leading to the implementation of the state plan. Because this plan was itself a response to the political pressures arising from the general perception that teacher education needed reforming, many felt that it was politically unwise to grant exceptions to it.

However, several members of the legislature and the Governor's Educational Liaison Officer were receptive to the idea of a serious, high-quality alternative to the state plan. After two years of negotiations, the Professional Standards Board and university officials developed a compromise that is embodied in Tulsa's teacher education program. That compromise, says Parr, has not only led to a marriage of the liberal arts and education at Tulsa but also has stimulated discussions about these issues on campuses across the state.

For more information, contact Warren Hipsher, Chair, Faculty of Education, University of Tulsa, 600 S. College, Tulsa, Okla. 74104.

RESOURCE ORGANIZATIONS

Listed below are selected organizations that sponsor efforts to improve the postsecondary preparation of teachers. Readers may contact them directly for further information.

American Association for Higher Education (AAHE)
Presidents' Forum on Teaching As a Profession
Russell Edgerton
President, AAHE
One Dupont Circle, Suite 600
Washington, DC 20036

American Association of Colleges for Teacher Education (AACTE)
David Imig
Executive Director, AACTE
One Dupont Circle, Suite 610
Washington, DC 20036
☐ *Association of Colleges and Schools of Education in State Universities and Land-Grant Colleges/and Affiliated Private Universities (ACSESULGC/ APU)*

☐ *Association of Independent Liberal Arts Colleges for Teacher Education (AILACTE)*
☐ *Teacher Education Council of State Colleges and Universities (TECSCU)*

American Association of State Colleges and Universities (AASCU)
Michael Mulnix
Director, Office of Public Affairs
One Dupont Circle, Suite 700
Washington, DC 20036
Task Force on Minority Teaching
Louis Barci
Program Associate, Academic Programs

American Council on Education (ACE)
Office of Minority Concerns
Reginald Wilson
Senior Scholar, Office of Minority Concerns
One Dupont Circle, Suite 800
Washington, DC 20036

The College Board
Donald Stewart
President
45 Columbus Avenue
New York, NY 10023

**Consortium for Excellence in
Teacher Education**
Eva Travers
CETE Coordinator
Swarthmore College
Swarthmore, PA 19081

Council for Basic Education
Ruth Mitchell
Associate Director
725 15th Street, NW
Washington, DC 20005

**Council of Chief State School
Officers**
Jon Quam
Director
School/College Collaboration
400 North Capitol Street, NW
Washington, DC 20001

**Education Commission of the States
(ECS)**
Barbara Holmes
Director of Teacher Education
1860 Lincoln Street, Suite 300
Denver, CO 80295

Educational Testing Service (ETS)
Gregory Anrig
President
Rosedale Road
Princeton, NJ 08541

The Holmes Group
Dr. Bradley West
Assistant to the President
501 Erickson Hall
Michigan State University
East Lansing, MI 48824

**National Association of State
Universities and Land-Grant
Colleges (NASULGC)**
Bob Aaron
Director of Communication Services
One Dupont Circle, Suite 718
Washington, DC 20036

**National Board for Professional
Teaching Standards**
Joan Baratz-Snowden
Vice President for Assessment and
Research
1320 18th Street, NW, Suite 401
Washington, DC 20036

**National Center for Research on
Teacher Education**
Mary Kennedy
Director
116 Erickson Hall
Michigan State University
East Lansing, MI 48824

National Center for the Paideia Program
Patricia Weiss
Director
NCNB Plaza, Suite 504
137 East Franklin Street, CB# 8040
University of North Carolina
Chapel Hill, NC 27599

National Council for Accreditation of Teacher Education (NCATE)
Richard Kunkel
Executive Director
2029 K Street, NW, Suite 500
Washington, DC 20006

National Governors' Association
Raymond C. Sheppach
Executive Director
Hall of the States
444 North Capitol Street, NW
Washington, DC 20001

Project 30
Daniel Fallon
Co-Director
P.O. Box F-1
College Station, TX 77844

Rand Corporation
Arthur Wise
Director
Center for the Study of the
Teaching Profession
2100 M Street, NW
Washington, DC 20037

U.S. Department of Education
Office of Educational Research and Improvement (OERI)
Elizabeth A. Ashburn
Senior Research Associate
Room 627-I
555 New Jersey Avenue, NW
Washington, DC 20208

NOTES

Chapter 1. Introduction

1. The National Commission on Excellence in Education, *A Nation at Risk* (Washington, D.C.: U.S. Department of Education, 1983).

2. Willis D. Hawley, Anne E. Austin, and Elizabeth S. Goldman, "Changing the Education of Teachers" (Nashville, Tenn.: Southern Regional Education Board, in press), 5.

3. "Education Majors Lack Solid Coursework, Says New SREB Study," *Higher Education Daily*, 25 June 1985, 2.

4. Holmes Group Executive Board, *Tomorrow's Teachers: A Report of the Holmes Group* (East Lansing, Mich.: The Holmes Group, 1986). Task Force on Teaching as a Profession, *A Nation Prepared: Teachers for the 21st Century* (New York: The Carnegie Forum on Education and the Economy, 1986).

5. C. Peter Magrath, "Causes for Concern About Teacher Education," in *Strengthening Teacher Education*, C. Peter Magrath, Robert L. Egbert, and associates (San Francisco: Jossey-Bass, 1987), 11.

Chapter 2. A Shortage of Quality

6. These include the National Association of State Teacher Education Certification; the National Center for Education Statistics in the Department of Education's Office for Educational Research and Improvement; the American Federation of Teachers; the National Education Association; the National Council for the Accreditation of Teacher Education; the American Association of Colleges for Teacher Education; the National Center for Education Information; the Carnegie Foundation for the Advancement of Teaching; and the Educational Testing Service.

7. Steven Prokesch, "Mounting Competition For College Teachers," *New York Times Education Life*, 12 April 1987, 30.

8. David Imig and Douglas Imig, "Strengthening and Maintaining the Pool of Qualified Teachers," in *Strengthening Teacher Education*, Magrath, Egbert, et al., 46–47.

9. C. Emily Feistritzer, *Teacher Supply and Demand Surveys 1988* (Washington, D.C.: National Center for Education Information, 1988).

10. Joyce D. Stern, ed., *The Condition of Education: Elementary and Secondary Education 1988*, Vol. 1 (Washington, D.C.: U.S. Department of Education, 1988), 104.

11. Joseph Berger, "Allure of Teaching Reviving; Education School Rolls Surge," *New York Times*, 6 May 1988, 1.

12. Alexander W. Astin, et al., *The American Freshman: National Norms for Fall 1988* (Los Angeles: American Council on Education, 1988), 5.

13. The Holmes Group, *Forum* 1 (n.d.): 7.

14. Judith E. Lanier and Judith W. Little, "Research on Teacher Education," in *Handbook of Research on Teaching*, 3rd ed., ed. Merlin C. Wittrock (New York: Macmillan, 1986), 538.

15. Arthur N. Applebee, Judith A. Langer, and Ina V.S. Mullis, *Literature and U.S. History: The Instructional Experience and Factual Knowledge of High School Juniors* (Princeton, N.J.: Educational Testing Service, 1987), 3.

16. *Ibid.*

17. John A. Dossey, et al., *Mathematics: Are We Measuring Up? The Mathematics Report Card*, executive summary (Princeton, N.J.: Educational Testing Service, 1988), 3.

18. *Ibid.*, 15.

19. Edward B. Fiske, "Back-to-Basics in Education Produces Gains in Arithmetic," *New York Times*, 8 June 1988, 1.

20. Dossey, *Mathematics*, 15.

21. Albert Shanker, quoted in "Study: Teens Weak in Science," *Capital* (Annapolis, Md.), 24 September 1988, 10. Bassam Shakhashiri, quoted in Joseph Berger, "U.S. Pupils Get Low Mark in Science," *New York Times*, 23 September 1988, A24. Ina V.S. Mullis and Lynn B. Jenkins, *The Science Report Card: Elements of Risk and Recovery* (Princeton, N.J.: Educational Testing Service, 1988).

22. Mullis and Jenkins, *The Science Report Card*, 5–6.

23. Cited in *Investment for the Future* (Washington, D.C.: Coalition for National Science Funding, 1988), 7.

24. Cited in Lee A. Daniels, "Finding New Ways to Make Geography Exciting," *New York Times*, 3 August 1988, B6.

25. Fiske, "Back-to-Basics," 1.

26. Cited in Barbara Vobejda, "U.S. Students Called Economic Illiterates," *Washington Post*, 29 December 1988, E1.

27. Albert Einstein quoted in Susan Poulsen Krogh, "How Not to Teach Science or Why Don't We Ever Cut up Frogs Any More?" *Wingspread Journal Special Report* 10 (July 1988): 1.

28. Cited in Edward B. Fiske, "America's Test Mania," *New York Times Education Supplement*, 10 April 1988, 20. See Kenneth A. Sirotnik, "What You See is

What You Get: Consistency, Persistency and Mediocrity in Classrooms," *Harvard Educational Review*, 53 (1983): 16–31, and John I. Goodlad, "School University Partnerships: Promises and Caveats," in *Partnership for Excellence: School/College Collaboration and Building Integrated Teacher Education Systems Statewide*, ed. Rebecca Yount (Washington, D.C.: Council of Chief State School Officers, 1985), 163–64.

29. Cited in William B. Boyd, "Connections Sought Between Needs of Kids and School Reform," *Wingspread Journal* 10 (July 1988): 1.

30. William Honig, quoted in David S. Wilson, "California Dropping Dick and Jane," *New York Times*, 18 October 1987, 10.

31. Harriet Tyson-Bernstein, "A Conspiracy of Good Intentions: America's Textbook Fiasco," executive summary, *Basic Education* 32 (April 1988): 2–3.

32. Fred M. Hechinger, "Learning by Rote," *New York Times*, 28 October 1986, C5. Lynne V. Cheney, *American Memory: A Report on the Humanities in the Nation's Public Schools* (Washington, D.C.: National Endowment for the Humanities, 1987), 22.

33. Dossey, et al., *Mathematics*, 5.

34. John A. Dossey, quoted in Edward B. Fiske, "Lessons," *New York Times*, 15 June 1988, B8.

35. Fiske, "Lessons," B8.

36. Dossey, et al., *Mathematics*, 5.

37. Edward B. Fiske, "Searching for the Key to Science Literacy," *New York Times Education Supplement*, 4 January 1987, 22.

38. Cited in Boyce Rensberger and Bar-

bara Vobejda, "Lab Work Evaporating from Schools," *Washington Post*, 21 November 1988, A1.

39. Iris Weiss, *Report of the 1985–86 National Survey of Science and Mathematics Education* (Research Triangle, N.C.: Research Triangle Institute, 1987), cited in Mullis, *Science Report Card*, 67.

40. Fiske, "Searching for the Key to Science Literacy," E21.

41. Malcolm W. Browne, "In Math, the Language of Science, Americans Grow Even Weaker," *New York Times*, 30 October 1988, D7. Fiske, "Searching for the Key to Science Literacy," E21.

42. Fiske, "Searching for the Key to Science Literacy," 22.

43. Applebee, Langer, and Mullis, *Literature and U.S. History*, 34.

44. *Ibid.*

45. Christopher Salter and Gilbert M. Grosvenor, quoted in Daniels, "Finding New Ways to Make Geography Exciting," B6.

46. "Survey Says More Teachers Hold Advanced Degrees," *Higher Education and National Affairs*, 13 July 1987, 12.

47. Carnegie Foundation for the Advancement of Teaching, "Prospective Teachers: Career Choices," *Change* 19 (March/April 1987): 32 (Tables 1 and 2). In 1984, seven out of ten of the newly certified earned their degrees in education; slightly more than one in ten took degrees in other nonliberal arts fields.

48. Eva C. Galambos, *Teacher Preparation: The Anatomy of a College Degree* (Atlanta, Ga.: Southern Regional Education Board, 1985). The study has been criticized for focusing on an unrepresentative sample of institutions, and its find-

ings may not reflect the realities in other regions.

49. Weiss, *1985–86 National Survey of Science and Mathematics Education*, cited in *Science Education News* 6 (March 1988): 1.

50. *A Summary of Data Collected From Graduate Record Examinations Test Takers During 1986–1987: Data Summary Report #12* (Princeton, N.J.: Educational Testing Service, 1988), Tables 33, 35, 37. The number of test takers was substantial: a total of 123,280 of whom 22,219 intended master's level study in education.

51. *Ibid.*

52. See Phillip Schlectly, as cited in *Partnership for Excellence*, ed. Yount, 178.

53. Lanier and Little, "Research on Teacher Education," 539–540 and 545. Explaining a pattern of "too many lows and progressively fewer highs" (page 540), they summarize data from the late 1970s on the SAT verbal and math scores. Eleven percent of the college students scoring in the top quintile went into teacher education in 1976–1979 and approximately 7 percent assumed teaching positions. By contrast, 38 percent of those in the lowest quintile pursued education majors and approximately 28 percent obtained teaching positions (page 539).

54. *Ibid.*, 545. For a different interpretation of the data on attrition, see Barbara Heyns, "Educational Defectors: A First Look at Teacher Attrition in the NLS-72," *Educational Researcher* (April 1988): 24–31.

55. Lanier and Little, "Research on Teacher Education," 540.

56. Linda Darling-Hammond and Barnett Berry, *The Evolution of Teacher Policy*

(The Rand Corporation, JRE-01, March 1988), 4. Stern, ed., *The Condition of Education*, Vol. 1, 21.

57. Ted Marchese, "Bulletin Board," *AAHE Bulletin* 42 (November 1988): 15.

58. Willis D. Hawley, "Toward a Comprehensive Strategy for Addressing the Teacher Shortage," *Phi Delta Kappan* 10 (June 1986): 712. Russell Edgerton, "Help Wanted: 'Education Presidents,'" *AAHE Bulletin* 41 (November 1988): 9.

59. *Results in Education: 1988* (Washington, D.C.: National Governors' Association, 1988), 14. Edgerton, "Help Wanted," 9.

60. Research About Teacher Education Project, *Teaching Teachers: Facts and Figures* (Washington, D.C.: AACTE, 1987), 37–45.

61. "Able Students Going Into Teaching: AACTE," *Phi Delta Kappan* (April 1987): 636.

62. Kenneth Howey and Nancy Zimpher, "Case Studies of Six Effective Teacher Education Programs in the Midwest," presentation at Association of Independent Liberal Arts Colleges for Teacher Education (AILACTE) annual conference, Davenport, Iowa, 1987.

63. Howey and Zimpher, "Case Studies." Carnegie Foundation for the Advancement of Teaching, "Future Teachers: Will There Be Enough Good Ones?" *Change* (September/October 1986): 29.

64. Alan R. Tom, "What are the Fundamental Problems in the Professional Education of Teachers?" in *Excellence in Teacher Education Through the Liberal Arts*, ed. Michael Carbone and Ann Wonsiewicz (Allentown, Pa.: Muhlenberg College, 1987), 29. Lanier and Little, "Research on Teacher Education," 542.

65. Astin, *The American Freshman*, 5. The all-time high was recorded in 1968, when the Vietnam conflict made a teaching deferment attractive to many students. It is doubtful, however, that the intentions of first-year students—on whom the Astin survey focuses—were so skewed by that event as to account for the disparities between the results reported then and now.

66. *Ibid.*, 5–6.

67. *Ibid.*, 6.

68. Ronald D. Opp, "A Twenty-Two Year Historical Trend Analysis of Characteristics of Prospective Teachers," paper presented to AACTE annual meeting, New Orleans, Louisiana, 1988, 4–7 and 29.

69. Astin, *The American Freshman*, 71 and 87.

70. Jerilee Grandy, *Trends in SAT Scores and Other Characteristics of Examinees Planning to Major in Mathematics, Science, or Engineering* (Princeton, N.J.: Educational Testing Service, 1989), Tables 20A and 22A. The objection is sometimes made that such SAT results present an unfairly negative picture, since they include the scores and self-reported class rank of many students who will never gain admission to a college or teacher education program. The objection has some merit given the recent and widespread imposition of education program entry standards. Nonetheless, the same distortion can be expected across all cohorts, and in the case of fields that are relatively selective, such as science or engineering, it is if anything likely to be more severe. In addition, as we shall see in Chapter Three, these orderings of

SAT scores for cohorts intending different majors agree broadly with orderings reported on the GRE for cohorts actually completing these (or similar) majors.

71. Grandy, *Trends in SAT Scores*, 25A.

72. Ernest L. Boyer, "Some Preliminary Findings of the Study: 'College: A Report on the Undergraduate Experience in America,'" in *Partnership for Excellence*, ed. Yount, 27.

Chapter 3. Expanding the Pool

73. *Chronicle of Higher Education*, 3 September 1986, 10.

74. National Commission for Excellence in Teacher Education, *A Call for Change in Teacher Education* (Washington, D.C.: AACTE, 1985), 26.

75. Task Force on Teaching as a Profession, *A Nation Prepared*, as excerpted in *Chronicle of Higher Education*, 21 May 1986, A47.

76. Gene I. Maeroff, "Power in the Classroom," *Foundation News* 29 (July/August 1988): 43. Thomas J. Lasley and Joseph F. Fogus, "Overview: The Themes of Reform," in *The Dynamics of Change in Teacher Education*, Vol. 1, ed. Thomas J. Lasley (Washington, D.C.: AACTE, 1986) 2.

77. Helen Featherstone, "A Time to Learn: The First Year of Teaching," *Colloquy* 1 (Spring 1988): 2. Conditions like these, of course, not only discourage those who might consider teaching; they create school environments inimical to student learning. Groups dedicated to "restructuring" the schools—such as the Coalition for Essential Schools, led by Theodore Sizer—are targeting, in particular, large schools, large classes, six- to

seven-period days, and curricula conceived on strict disciplinary lines and strongly emphasizing coverage. They are breaking large schools into smaller units and large classes into seminars; providing teachers more time with fewer students; encouraging in-depth study and reflection by focusing on fewer, but essential, subjects; providing students more common intellectual experience; and encouraging teachers to "coach" more and lecture less. See Theodore R. Sizer, *Horace's Compromise* (Boston: Houghton Mifflin, 1984).

78. Magrath, "Causes for Concern About Teacher Education," 11.

79. *Carnegie Foundation News*, 11 September 1988, 1.

80. *Carnegie Foundation News*, 22 May 1988, 1.

81. Edward B. Fiske, "Lessons," B6.

82. Samuel Weiss, "Panel to Urge a Broader Role for Teachers," *New York Times*, 11 March 1988, B1. See also Richard M. Brandt, "Initiatives and Issues in Teacher Education," *Connections* 3 (Fall 1988): 6.

83. Robert A. Roth, "Emergency Certificates, Misassignment of Teachers, and Other 'Dirty Little Secrets,'" *Phi Delta Kappan* 67 (June 1986): 725–727. NCETE, *A Call for Change*, 18.

84. William J. Warren, "Alternative Certificates: New Paths to Teaching," *New York Times*, 28 September 1988, B15.

85. Lynn Olson, "Alternative Certification Routes Praised," *Education Week*, 11 March 1987, 5.

86. "Teacher Wisdom," *New York Times*, 21 August 1986, B7.

87. Warren, "Alternative Certificates,"

B15.

88. Even "national" universities that draw few students from local schools can learn from these kinds of involvements, and they can perform an important service by putting their prestige behind this larger professional cause.

89. As an example of the common tendency to assume that future teachers must major in education, see columnist William Raspberry writing on the impact of the new National Board for Professional Teaching Standards: "But it's hard to see how board certification...would inspire bright college students to switch their majors to education.... " ("Will National Certification Make Better Teachers?" Annapolis [Md.] *Capital*, 10 July 1989, 10).

90. Astin, *The American Freshman*, 6.

91. Stern, ed., *The Condition of Education: Postsecondary Education 1988*, Vol. 2, 20 and 64–66.

92. "Degrees and Other Formal Awards Conferred, 1984-85" (Washington, D.C.: U.S. Department of Education, Center for Education Statistics, 1987), Table 183.

93. See also note 70.

94. Bernard R. Gifford and John E. King, "Should We Abolish the Bachelors Degree in Education?" *Change* 18 (September/October 1986): 35.

95. Lanier and Little, "Research on Teacher Education," 540.

96. Fran Teplitz, "Teacher Supply and Recruitment," unpublished background paper for Edward W. Hazen Foundation, 4.

97. Gifford and King, "Should We Abolish the Bachelors Degree in Education?" 35.

Chapter 4. A Liberal and Professional Education

98. James B. Conant, *The Child, the Parent, and the State* (Cambridge, Mass.: Harvard University Press, 1959), 1, quoted in *College*, Boyer, 58.

99. The Educational Leadership Project, *Liberal Education: A Concept for American High Schools* (New York: Christian A. Johnson Endeavor Foundation, 1988).

100. *Ibid.*, 2.

101. Jaime Escalante's achievement in teaching calculus to Hispanic students in East Los Angeles is but the best-known example of what can be done "against the odds" when powerful teaching combines with high expectations.

102. Lauren B. Resnick, *Education and Learning to Think* (Washington, D.C.: National Academy Press, 1988). Diane Ravitch, "Education and the Public Good," *College Board Review* 148 (Summer 1988): 11ff.

103. Ravitch, "Education and the Public Good," 37.

104. Donna H. Kerr, "Authority and Responsibility in Public Schooling," in *86th Yearbook, Part 1: The Ecology of School Renewal*, ed. John I. Goodlad (Chicago: National Society for the Study of Education, 1987), 22–25, as cited in John I. Goodlad, "Studying the Education of Educators: Value-Driven Inquiry," *Phi Delta Kappan* 70 (October 1988): 109.

105. Daniel Fallon, presentation at AAHE annual meeting, Washington, D.C., 1988.

106. Holmes Group Executive Board, *Tomorrow's Teachers*, 47.

107. Gary Sykes, quoted in The Holmes Group, *Forum* 1 (n.d.): 11.

108. Alan R. Tom, "The Case for Maintaining Teacher Education at the Undergraduate Level," report prepared for the Coalition of Teacher Education Programs (1985, revised March 1986), 15.

109. Charles Karelis, presentation at AAHE annual meeting, Chicago, Illinois, 1987.

110. Fallon, presentation at AAHE annual meeting, 1988.

111. R. S. Peters, quoted in Maxine Greene, "Liberal Learning and Teacher Education," in Excellence in Teacher Education, ed. Carbone and Wonsiewicz, 23.

112. Greene, "Liberal Learning and Teacher Education," 23. See also Hugh G. Petrie, "The Liberal Arts and Sciences in the Teacher Education Curriculum," in Excellence in Teacher Education, ed. Carbone and Wonsiewicz, 41.

113. Holmes Group Executive Board, Tomorrow's Teachers, 48.

114. Edward J. Meade, Jr., "Recent Reports on Education: Some Implications for Preparing Teachers," in Issues in Teacher Education, vol. 2, ed. Thomas J. Lasley (Washington, D.C.: AACTE, 1986), 75.

115. Robert Shoenberg, presentation at AAC annual meeting, Washington, D.C., 1989.

116. John Dewey, as cited in Norma Nutter, "Defining the Excellent Teacher Preparation Program," in Issues in Teacher Education, vol. 2, ed. Lasley, 120.

117. See Dennis O'Brien, "The Importance of Higher Education to Teacher Effectiveness," in Strengthening Teacher Education, Magrath, et al., 26.

118. Martin Haberman, "An Evaluation of the Rationale for Required Teacher Education: Beginning Teachers With and Without Teacher Preparation," in Issues in Teacher Education, Vol. 2, ed. Lasley, 34.

119. Edith E. Baldwin, "Theory vs. Ideology in the Practice of Teacher Education," The Journal of Teacher Education 38 (January-February, 1987): 18-19. Rodman B. Webb and Robert R. Sherman, "Liberal Education: An Aim for Colleges of Education," The Journal of Teacher Education 34 (July-August 1983): 23-26.

120. David C. Smith, "Redesigning the Curriculum in Teacher Education," in Strengthening Teacher Education, Magrath, et al., 91-92. Willis D. Hawley, "Notes on the Redesign of Teacher Education," presentation at Southeast Regional Forum of ECS, Tampa, Florida, 1986, 2.

121. Willis D. Hawley, quoted in Jack McCurdy, "Teacher-Education Reforms Move Ahead, but Movement Faces Skeptics and Problems," Chronicle of Higher Education, 27 May 1987, 23.

122. Lee S. Shulman, "Knowledge and Teaching: Foundations of the New Reform," Harvard Educational Review, 57 (February 1987): 8.

123. Frank Murray, presentation to AAHE annual meeting, Washington, D.C., 1988.

124. Ibid., quoting St. Augustine.

125. Shoenberg, presentation at AAC annual meeting, 1989.

126. Don Davies, "Foreword," in The Liberal Arts and Teacher Education: A Confrontation, ed. Donald N. Bigelow (Lincoln, Nebr.: University of Nebraska Press, 1971), xi.

127. John Palmer, cited in The Holmes Group, Forum, 1 (n.d.): 5.

128. See Jerome Bruner, quoted in Eva Foldes Travers, "Rally 'Round the Liberal Arts: And Pedagogy Comes Tumbling After," NEH-CETE Conference on Teacher Education and the Liberal Arts, Breadloaf, Vermont, 1987, 11. See also Carl Schorske, quoted in Boyer, College, 151.

129. Jerome S. Bruner, On Knowing (Cambridge, Mass.: Harvard University Press, 1963), 83.

130. Penelope L. Peterson, "Teachers' and Students' Cognitional Knowledge for Classroom Teaching and Learning," Educational Researcher 17 (June/July 1988): 5.

131. Webb and Sherman, "Liberal Education: An Aim for Colleges of Education," 24.

132. A. N. Whitehead, quoted in Ernest A. Lynton and Sandra E. Elman, New Priorities for the University: Meeting Society's Needs for Applied Knowledge and Competent Individuals (San Francisco: Jossey-Bass, 1987), 57.

Chapter 5. Extended, Sequentially Structured Programs

133. See Alan R. Tom, "The Holmes Group Report: Its Latent Political Agenda," Teachers College Record 88 (Spring 1987): 430–435, and Robert L. Jacobson, "Some College Officials Balk at Proposals to Drop Education Majors," Chronicle of Higher Education, 18 June 1986, 23.

134. Judith Lanier, "A Look at the Research/Demographics: What Do They Tell Us About Integrating Statewide Systems for Teacher Education?" in Partnership for Excellence, 18.

135. Judith Lanier, presentation at AAHE annual meeting, Washington, D.C., 1988.

136. Ibid.

137. Beverly T. Watkins, "Mixed Results Seen in Universities' Reform of Teacher Education," Chronicle of Higher Education, 22 February 1989, A20. Robert Shoenberg, personal communication to authors. See also Work in Progress: The Holmes Group One Year On (East Lansing, Mich.: The Holmes Group, 1989).

138. Maxine Greene, "Perspectives and Visions: Rationale for 'Foundations' in Teacher Education," in New Directions in Teacher Education: Foundations, Curriculum, Policy, ed. Jon Denton, et al. (College Station, Tex.: Texas A&M University Press, 1984), 3–4.

139. Alan R. Tom, How Should Teachers Be Educated: An Assessment of Three Reform Reports (Bloomington, Ind.: Phi Delta Kappa Educational Foundation, 1987), 29. If only in one sentence, the Carnegie report does acknowledge that there might be acceptable alternatives, at least to sequential preparation.

140. Arthur E. Wise, "If We are Ever to 'Professionalize' Schoolteaching, Universities Must Redesign Education Programs," Chronicle of Higher Education, 16 November 1988, B1. William E. Gardner, quoted in Jean Evangelauf, "School-Reform Drive Spotlights Colleges' Education of Teachers," Chronicle of Higher Education, 2 September 1987, A48.

141. Edith Guyton and George Antonelli, "Educational Leaders' Reports of Priorities and Activities in Selected Areas of Teacher Education Reform," Journal of Teacher Education 38 (May/June 1987): 45–49.

142. William E. Gardner, "President's Briefing," *AACTE Briefs* 8 (August 1987): 16. Robert Richardson, "Education-College Deans Respond to Recent National Reports," *Journal of General Education* 38 (1987): 249–261.

143. Tom, "What are the Fundamental Problems in the Professional Education of Teachers?" 28.

144. Holmes Group Executive Board, *Tomorrow's Teachers*, 52. D. C. Berliner, "Making the Right Changes in Preservice Education," *Phi Delta Kappan* 66 (October 1984): 94–96. See also Edward Bristow, "Are Teacher Colleges Destroying American Education?" *The College Board Review* 142 (Winter 1986): 49.

145. This effort to assemble a "knowledge base"–traditionally an area of weakness–is important. That there is deep disagreement about its content is not, as some critics would have it, an indication of the discipline's "problematic status." If it were, we should need to be equally concerned with some other disciplines–English and foreign languages perhaps foremost among them–that are at least as divided on fundamental issues of what they can know.

146. Lanier and Little, "Research on Teacher Education," 555.

147. Tom, *How Should Teachers Be Educated?* 23–25.

148. Joseph Gore, "Liberal and Professional Education: Keep Them Separate," *Journal of Teacher Education* 38 (January/February 1987): 4. The same wish to establish education as an authentic discipline by separating it from the liberal arts underlies another dean's proposals in the June 1986 issue of *Phi Delta Kap-*

pan (722). Focusing on how the awarding of teaching licenses must be changed, he proposes first that license examinations given to baccalaureate recipients "test arcane knowledge and vocabulary." Every profession "uses a technical language unfamiliar to the public," he points out with apparent exasperation, yet "professional educators do just the reverse; they try to communicate at about a fourth-grade level in order to be understood by the public at large." His second proposal addresses the supposed problem that "many liberal arts majors do as well as education majors on certification examinations" because in their liberal arts courses they have studied what he admits to being various kinds of "professional content," including oral communication, computer literacy, effective writing, creative thinking, problem solving, and organizational theory and behavior. "Such content, no matter how valuable [it is]," he continues, "should be identified and removed from . . . [the] examinations. Not to do so will guarantee that increasing numbers of liberal arts graduates will continue to pass professional examinations for teachers and will reinforce the perception that teaching has no body of knowledge to call its own."

149. O'Brien, "The Importance of Higher Education," 23.

150. Thomas J. Lasley and Joseph F. Rogus, "Overview: The Themes of Reform," in *The Dynamics of Change in Teacher Education*, Vol. 1, ed. Lasley, 7. Webb and Sherman, "Liberal Education: An Aim for Colleges of Education," 23. Robert N. Bush, "Teacher Education Re-

form: Lessons From the Past Half Centu-ry," *Journal of Teacher Education* 38 (May/June 1987): 16.

151. Edward R. Ducharme, "Developing Existing Education Faculty," in *Strengthening Teacher Education*, ed. Magrath et al., 78.

152. Nutter, "Defining the Excellent Teacher Preparation Program," in *Issues in Teacher Education* Vol. 2, ed. Lasley, 124.

153. Ducharme, "Developing Existing Education Faculty," 78.

154. Lanier and Little, "Research on Teacher Education," 531.

155. Smith, " Redesigning the Curriculum in Teacher Education," 96.

156. Lanier, "A Look at the Research/Demographics," 16. See also Gary Sykes, quoted in Watkins, "Mixed Results Seen in Universities' Efforts," A20.

157. Joan S. Stark and Malcolm A. Lowther, *Strengthening the Ties That Bind: Integrating Undergraduate Liberal and Professional Study* (Ann Arbor, Mich.: University of Michigan Press, 1988), 1.

158. Marcia J. Keith, "We've Heard This Song...Or Have We?" *Journal of Teacher Education* 38 (May-June 1987): 23.

159. Gerald Graff, "What Should We Be Teaching–When There's No 'We'?" *The Yale Journal of Criticism* 1 (1987): 204.

160. Travers, "Rally 'Round the Liberal Arts," 16.

161. From progress reports from campus examiners in the AAC project, "Using External Examiners to Assess Learning in Arts and Sciences Majors."

162. William H. Newell, "Interdisciplinary Studies are Alive and Well," *AAHE Bulletin* 40 (April 1988): 10–12.

163. Zelda F. Gamson and associates, *Liberating Education* (San Francisco: Jossey-Bass, 1984), 126.

164. Tom, *How Should Teachers Be Educated?* 16.

165. Linda Bunnell Jones, "Building Campus-Wide Support for Teacher Education," in *Strengthening Teacher Education*, ed. Magrath et al., 126.

166. Tom, *How Should Teachers Be Educated?* 24–25. According to Gary Sykes of the Holmes Group, early evidence from institutions that already have converted to five-year programs suggests that "there may be some initial drop in enrollment, but it soon picks up again." (*Chronicle of Higher Education*, 22 February 1989, A20.) It is unclear, however, whether this result–which one might predict at institutions serving the upper tiers of the student market–could be expected at colleges and universities more typical of those preparing the nation's teachers.

Chapter 6. Intellectual Impediments to Integration

167. Merle Borrowman, "About Professors of Education," in *The Professor of Education: An Assessment of Conditions*, ed. Ayres Bagley (Minneapolis, Minn.: University of Minnesota Press, 1975), 60.

168. Michael J. Baxter, "The Action Stage," *System* 24 (September 1988): 14.

169. David Perkins, "We Teach the Books We Have Already Written," *Chronicle of Higher Education*, 7 September 1988, B10.

170. Boyer, *College*, 237, Table 43.

171. *Integrity in the College Curriculum: A Report to the Academic Community* (Wash-

ington, D.C.: Association of American Colleges, 1985), 4.

172. *Ibid.*, 38.

173. Harriet W. Sheridan, "The Compleat Professor, Jr.," *AAHE Bulletin* 41 (December 1988): 3.

174. *Integrity*, 10.

175. K. Patricia Cross, "In Search of Zippers," *AAHE Bulletin* 40 (June 1988): 4.

176. Edward B. Fiske, "Lessons," *AACTE Briefs* 9 (June 1988): 5.

177. Merrill D. Peterson, "The University and the Larger Community, in *The Humanities in the University: Strategies for the 1990's*, W. R. Connor, et al. (New York: ACLS, 1988), 6.

178. Richard S. Podemski and John N. Mangieri, "Professional Service–A Skewed Reward," *Educational Horizons* 65 (Winter 1987): 67–70.

179. John Gardner, quoted in Harland Cleveland, "Prospects for a New Integrative Vision," *AAHE Bulletin* 40 (May 1988): 12.

180. *Ibid.*, 11.

181. Jean A. King, "The Uneasy Relationship between Teacher Education and the Liberal Arts and Sciences," *Journal of Teacher Education* 38 (January-February 1987): 6–7.

182. Edwin J. Meyer, "A Radical Proposal for Teacher Preparation," *Phi Delta Kappan* 67 (June 1986): 92.

183. David S. Martin, "Professional Credibility Through Wider Links," *Educational Horizons* 65 (Winter 1987): 56. King, "The Uneasy Relationship," 7.

184. John Goodlad, cited in Jones, "Teacher Education," 49.

185. Louis Albert, "AAHE Leads Two New Efforts to Strengthen the Teaching Profession," *AAHE Bulletin* 40 (June 1988): 13.

186. "The Letter: 37 Presidents Write...." *AAHE Bulletin* 40 (November 1987): 14.

187. Susan Resneck Parr, "Teaching the Humanities in the University," in *The Humanities in the University*, Connor, et al., 11.

188. Don Davies in *The Liberal Arts and Teacher Education*, ed. Begelow, x.

189. The President's Commission on Higher Education, *Higher Education for American Democracy* Vol. 1 (Washington, D.C.: U.S. Government Printing Office, 1947), 74, quoted in *Strengthening the Ties That Bind*, Stark and Lowther, 42.

190. Eva Feldes Travers and Susan Riemer Sacks, *Teacher Education and the Liberal Arts: The Position of the Consortium for Excellence in Teacher Education* (CETE, 1987), 10–15.

191. Russell Edgerton, "All Roads Lead to Teaching," *AAHE Bulletin* 40 (April 1988): 9.

192. *Ibid.*

193. *Ibid.*

194. Travers, "Rally 'Round the Liberal Arts," 23.

195. See Burton R. Clark, "Schools of Education: The Academic-Professional Seesaw," *Change* 21 (January/February 1989): 60–62.

Chapter 7. Recommendations

196. W. Ann Reynolds, "What College and University Presidents Can Do to Strengthen Teacher Preparation," in *Strengthening Teacher Education*, Magrath, et al., 112.

197. Paul Woodring, "Too Bright to be a Teacher?" *Phi Delta Kappan* 68 (April

1987): 617–618.

198. Allan W. Ostar, *An Urgent Imperative*, (Washington, D.C.: AASCU, 1986), v.

199. *Ibid.*, 2–3.

200. Woodring, "Too Bright to be a Teacher?" 618.

201. King, *The Uneasy Relationship*, 6.

202. Reynolds, "What College and University Presidents Can Do," 104–105.

203. *Is the Education of Teachers Changing?* (Atlanta, Ga.: SREB, 1988), 7. Russell Edgerton, "Help Wanted: 'Education Presidents,'" *AAHE Bulletin* 41 (November 1988): 9. Willis Hawley, et al., *Changing the Education of Teachers* (paper prepared for SREB), 53.

204. Hawley, *Changing the Education of Teachers*, 50 and 64–65. C. Peter Magrath, "The Responsibility of the University in Building Collaborative and Integrative Systems for Teacher Education," in *Partnership for Excellence*, ed. Yount, 36.

205. Cited in Lee S. Shulman, "Learning to Teach," *AAHE Bulletin* 40 (November 1987): 6.

206. Carolyn M. Evertson, et al., "Making a Difference in Educational Quality Through Teacher Education," *Journal of Teacher Education* 36 (May/June 1985): 4. See also Goodlad, "School/University Partnerships," in *Partnerships for Excellence*, ed. Yount, 163.

207. Richard F. Elmore, "How We Teach is What We Teach," *AAHE Bulletin* 41 (April 1989): 11–14.

208. Quoted in Tommy Ehrbar, "The Opening of the American Mind," *Pitt Magazine* 32 (May 1988): 39.

209. Boyer, *College*, 126.

210. *Ibid*, 128.

211. Working Party on Effective State Action to Improve Undergraduate Education, *Transforming the State Role in Undergraduate Education: Time for a Different View* (Denver, Colo.: ECS, 1986), 19.

212. Ehrbar, "The Opening of the American Mind," 39.

213. Sheridan, "The Compleat Professor, Jr.," 5–6. Boyer, *College*, 156–157.

214. Stephen C. MacDonald, "Critical Thinking: 'Grokking the Fullness,'" *College Teaching* 36 (Summer 1988): 91–93.

215. Joseph Katz, et al., *A New Vitality in General Education*, (Washington, D.C.: AAC, 1988), 38.

216. *Ibid.*

217. *Integrity*, 12.

218. Cross, "Zippers," 7.

219. Katz, et al., *A New Vitality*, 37–39.

220. *Ibid*, 54.

221. Joseph Katz, "Turning Professors Into Teachers," *AAHE Bulletin* 41 (December 1988): 12. Katz, et al., *A New Vitality*, 36–37.

222. Edgerton, "All Roads Lead to Teaching," 8.

223. Katz, et al., *A New Vitality*, 37.

224. Alexander W. Astin, *Achieving Educational Excellence: A Critical Assessment of Priorities and Practices in Higher Education* (San Francisco: Jossey-Bass, 1985), 133, as quoted in *New Priorities for the University*, Lynton and Elman, 59.

225. Zelda F. Gamson and Patrick J. Hill, "Creating a Lively Academic Community," in *Liberating Education* (San Francisco: Jossey-Bass, 1984), Zelda F. Gamson et al., 94.

226. Lynton and Elman, *New Priorities*

for the University, 56–68.

227. Boyer, College, 43–57.

228. Katz, et al., A New Vitality, 43–45.

229. Boyer, College, 52.

230. Lynton and Elman, New Priorities for the University, 49–51.

231. Ibid., 51–52.

232. Michael Polanyi, The Tacit Dimension (Garden City, N.Y.: Doubleday, 1967), 72, as quoted in College, Boyer, 91. Edward Said, quoted in Greene, "Liberal Learning and Teacher Education," 23.

233. Cleveland, "Prospects for a New Integrative Vision," 12.

234. Graff, "What Should We Be Teaching," 204–207.

235. Ibid., 199.

236. Travers, "Rally 'Round the Liberal Arts," 16–17.

237. Carol G. Schneider, review of The Closing of the American Mind, by Allan Bloom, Thought and Action 4 (Fall 1988): 121.

238. Katz, et al., A New Vitality, 25–26.

239. Linda Bunnell Jones, "Teacher Education: An All-University Responsibility," in The Dynamics of Change in Teacher Education, Vol. 1, ed. Lasley, 51. Hawley, "Changing the Education of Teachers," 57. It is perhaps because of the ineffectiveness of these committees that reform to date has brought more change in teacher education than in the education of teachers—a campus-wide responsibility requiring articulation with the arts and sciences. (Willis Hawley, quoted in David C. Imig, "Briefing," AACTE Briefs 9 [May 1988]: 7)

240. Jones, "Building Campus-Wide Support for Teacher Education," 133. Commission for Educational Quality,

Improving Teacher Education: An Agenda for Higher Education and the Schools (Atlanta, Ga.: SREB, 1985), 10. See also Renee T. Clift and Michael Say, "Teacher Education: Collaboration or Conflict?" Journal of Teacher Education 39 (May/June 1988): 2–7.

241. Jones, "Building Campus-Wide Support for Teacher Education," 134.

242. King, "The Uneasy Relationship," 8.

243. Scott Heller, "Universities Grapple with Academic Politics as They Strive to Change Their Curricula," Chronicle of Higher Education, 7 September 1988, A12.

244. Lynne V. Cheney, Humanities in America (Washington, D.C.: NEH, 1988), 5. Robert Zemsky, Structure and Coherence: Measuring the Undergraduate Curriculum (Washington, D.C.: AAC, 1989), 36–37.

245. Boyer, College, 43–57 and 83–101. See also Joseph S. Johnston, Jr., et al., Unfinished Design: The Humanities and Social Sciences in Undergraduate Engineering Education (Washington, D.C.: AAC, 1988), 30–31.

246. George F. Kneller, "The Proper Study of Education," in New Directions in Teacher Education, ed. Jon Denton, et al., 21–23.

247. Ibid., 23.

248. Ibid.

249. Roger Henry, personal communication quoted in Boyer, College, 216.

250. See Willis Hawley, quoted in Geraldine Joncich Clifford and James W. Guthrie, Ed School: A Brief for Professional Education (Chicago: University of Chicago Press, 1988), 357–358.

251. Rudy Perpich, interview with Rudy

Perpich and Frank Newman, "Partners in Learning," *AAHE Bulletin* 41 (November 1988): 5.

252. Ann M. Rule and Charles M. Stanton, "Excellence in Teacher Education: The Liberal Arts College Perspective," in *Teacher Education in Liberal Arts Settings: Achievements, Realities and Challenges*, ed. Alan R. Tom (Washington, D.C.: AACTE and AILACTE, 1985), 15.

253. Meade, "Recent Reports on Education," 76.

254. Kneller, "The Proper Study of Education," 13–24.

255. Charles Karelis, presentation at AAHE annual meeting, Chicago, Illinois, 1987.

256. Smith, "Redesigning the Curriculum in Teacher Education," 90. Jones, "Building Campus-Wide Suport," 132.

257. Tom Bird, Lee S. Shulman and Gary Sykes, "Ordinary People, Extraordinary Work: Notes on Schoolteaching at the Turn of the Century," in *The Schools We've Got, The Schools We Need*, ed. David G. Imig and Carol Smith (Washington, D.C.: AACTE and CCSSO, 1987), 72–73. Shulman, "Learning to Teach," 8–9.

258. Bernard R. Gifford in Gifford and King, "Should We Abolish the Bachelors Degree in Education?" 36.

259. Jones, "Building Campus-Wide Support," 132.

260. Ducharme, "Developing Existing Education Faculty," 79–80. John I. Goodlad, "School/University Partnerships: Promises and Caveats," in *Partnership for Excellence*, ed. Yount, 170.

261. Boyer, *College*, 109.

262. Petrie, "The Liberal Arts and Sciences in the Teacher Education Curriculum," 41.

263. Task Force on Teaching as a Profession, *A Nation Prepared*, as excerpted in *Chronicle of Higher Education*, 21 May 1986, A50.

264. Keith, "We've Heard This Song... Or Have We?" 20.

265. Research About Teacher Education Project, *Teaching Teachers*, 20–21.

266. J. Myron Atkin, "Reexamining the University's Role in Educating Teachers," in *Strengthening Teacher Education*, Magrath, 13.

267. Research About Teacher Education Project, *Teaching Teachers*, 18.

268. Tom, "What are the Fundamental Problems in the Professional Education of Teachers?" 29.

269. Jones, "Teacher Education," 51.

270. James D. Greenberg, "The Case for Teacher Education: Open and Shut," *Journal of Teacher Education* 34 (July-August 1983): 4.

271. Webb and Sherman, "Liberal Education," 24.

272. Lanier and Little, "Research on Teacher Education," 548.

273. Tom, "What are the Fundamental Problems in the Professional Education of Teachers?" 29. Commission for Educational Quality, *Improving Teacher Education*, 9.

274. Kneller, "The Proper Study of Education," 21. Commission for Educational Quality, *Improving Teacher Education*, 7.

275. For a number of the suggestions that follow here and in ensuing sections dealing with professional education, the authors are indebted to Ann Converse Shelly, a consultant to the AAC project.

276. Edward J. Meade, Jr. "Teaching: A Career of Choice," in *Excellence in Teacher Education Through the Liberal Arts*, ed. Carbone and Wonsiewicz, 21.
277. Galambos, *Teacher Preparation*, 26–27.
278. *Ibid.* E.I. Holmstrom, *Recent Changes in Teacher Education Programs* (Washington, D.C.: ACE, 1985), as cited in *The Evolution of Teacher Policy*, Darling-Hammond and Berry, 17–18.
279. Smith, "Redesigning the Curriculum in Teacher Education," 92.
280. Eva C. Galambos, "Common Directions Toward Improvement," in *Improving Teacher Education*, ed. Eva C. Galambos (San Francisco: Jossey-Bass, 1986), 95. Meade, "Recent Reports on Education," in *Issues in Teacher Education*, Lasley, 76.
281. Travers and Sacks, *Teacher Education and the Liberal Arts*, 12. See also "How It's Done at Dartmouth," interview with Faith Dunne in *Colloquy* 2 (Fall 1988): 17.
282. See Travers, "Rally 'Round the Liberal Arts," 22.
283. O'Brien, "The Importance of Higher Education to Teacher Effectiveness," 31.
284. Research About Teacher Education Project, *Teaching Teachers*, 12–14.
285. Cheney, *American Memory*, 22.
286. Alan R. Tom, "Fifth Year Teacher Preparation: A Solution in Search of a Problem," *The Forum for Liberal Education* 7 (November/December 1984): 3.
287. Lanier and Little, "Research on Teacher Education," 551.
288. Hawley, "Notes on the Redesign of Teacher Education," 4. Lasley and Rogus, "Overview: The Themes of Reform," 4.
289. Bush, "Teacher Education Reform," 16.
290. Lanier and Little, "Research on Teacher Education," 551.
291. Smith, "Redesigning the Curriculum in Teacher Education," 93.
292. Shulman, "Learning to Teach," 7.
293. Research About Teacher Education Project, *Teaching Teachers*, 14.
294. Kenneth R. Howey, "The Next Generation of Teacher Preparation Programs," in *The Dynamics of Change in Teacher Education*, ed. Lasley, 174.
295. Featherstone, "A Time to Learn," 4. Lasley, ed., *The Dynamics of Change in Teacher Education*, 14. Judith Lanier, "A Look at the Research/Demographics," 14.
296. Hillary B. Neuweiler, *Teacher Education in the States: 50-State Survey of Legislative and Administrative Actions* (Washington, D.C.: AACTE, 1987), v. Lanier and Little, "Research on Teacher Education," 561.
297. Evertson, et al., "Making a Difference," 8.
298. P. Michael Timpane, "Can Collaboration Advance Teacher Education?" in *Partnership for Excellence*, ed. Yount, 92.
299. Bird, Shulman, and Sykes in *The Schools We've Got*, ed. Imig and Smith, 78.
300. Featherstone, "A Time to Learn," 3–4.
301. "Improving the Selection of Teachers," *Research in Brief* IS87-108RIB (April 1987): 1.
302. *Ibid.*
303. Linda Darling-Hammond and Joslyn Green, "Teacher Quality and Educational Equality," *College Board Review* 148 (Summer 1988): 22.

304. *Ibid.*, 40.
305. John I. Goodlad, quoted in *AACTE Briefs* 7 (March-April 1986): 10.
306. Neuweiler, *Teacher Education in the States*, v.
307. Lanier and Little, "Research on Teacher Education," 548 and 562.
308. Cheney, *American Memory*, 23.
309. *Ibid.*
310. Maeroff, "Power in the Classroom," 43.
311. *Report to the President* (Washington, D.C.: President's Committee on the Arts and the Humanities, 1988), 12–13.
312. *Ibid.*, 13.
313. *...And Gladly Teach* (New York: The Ford Foundation, 1987), 7–9.
314. *Report to the President*, 14.
315. Lanier and Little, "Research on Teacher Education," 564.
316. Howard D. Mehlinger, "Simple but Radical Reform of Teacher Education," *Educational Horizons* 65 (Winter 1987): 59.
317. Courtney Leatherman, "Reforms in Education of Schoolteachers Face Tough New Challenge," *Chronicle of Higher Education*, 20 April 1988, A1.
318. Darling-Hammond and Berry, *The Evolution of Teacher Policy*, 14–17.
319. Stark and Lowther, *Strengthening the Ties That Bind*, 34.

Chapter 8. Educating Minority Students for Teaching
320. Dagmar Kauffman, ed., *Minority Teacher Recruitment and Retention: A Public Policy Issue* (Washington, D.C.: AACTE, 1988), 16.
321. The Commission on Minority Participation in Education and American

Life, *One Third of a Nation* (Washington, D.C.: ACE, 1988), 2–3.
322. "Report Signals Push for Minority Participation," *Higher Education and National Affairs*, 6 June 1988, 1.
323. Committee on Multicultural Education, *Minority Teacher Recruitment and Retention: A Call for Action* (Washington, D.C.: AACTE, 1987), 3.
324. "Status of the American Public School Teacher," 1987 National Education Association study cited in "Survey Says More Teachers Hold Advanced Degrees," *Higher Education and National Affairs*, 13 July 1987, 12.
325. Kauffman, ed., *Minority Teacher Recruitment and Retention*, 1.
326. Reginald Wilson and Deborah J. Carter, *Minorities in Higher Education: Seventh Annual Status Report* (Washington, D.C.: ACE, 1988), 16–17.
327. AACTE survey data cited in Elaine A. Witty, "Teacher Education: Lost Ground for Blacks," *NAFEO Inroads* 2 (February/March 1988): 7.
328. G. Pritchy Smith, quoted in Cheryl Fields, "Poor Test Scores Bar Many Minority Students from Teacher Training," *Chronicle of Higher Education*, 2 November 1988, A32.
329. Kauffmann, ed., *Minority Teacher Recruitment and Retention*, 14–15.
330. Task Force on Teaching as a Profession, *A Nation Prepared: Teachers for the 21st Century*, as excerpted in *Chronicle of Higher Education*, 21 May 1986, A51.
331. 1987 OERI data cited in Witty, "Teacher Education: Lost Ground for Blacks," 8.
332. Higher Education Research Program, "Seeing Straight Through a Mud-

dle," *Policy Perspectives* 1 (September 1988): 6.

333. Commission on Minority Participation in Education and American Life, *One-Third of a Nation*, 4–5.

334. Darling-Hammond and Green, "Teacher Quality and Educational Equality," 17.

335. Wilson and J. Carter, *Minorities in Higher Education: Seventh Annual Status Report*, 3. The figures cited are for the 18- to 24-year-old age cohort.

336. Commission on Minority Participation in Education and American Life, *One-Third of a Nation*, 5–6.

337. Reginald Wilson and Sarah E. Melendez, *Minorities in Higher Education: Sixth Annual Status Report* (Washington, D.C.: ACE, 1987), 3.

338. Kauffman, ed., *Minority Teacher Recruitment and Retention*, 16.

339. Opp, "A Twenty-Two-Year Historical Trend Analysis of Characteristics of Prospective Teachers," 9–11.

340. Kauffman, ed., *Minority Teacher Recruitment and Retention*, 16.

341. *Digest of Educational Statistics* (Washington, D.C.: Center for Educational Statistics, Office of Educational Research and Improvement, 1988), 245. For a variety of reasons, the graduation rates of students attending schools that enroll large numbers of minority students are noticeably better, and these schools account for minority college graduates in numbers disproportionate to their enrollments. For example, historically black colleges and universities (HBCUs), while enrolling only 18 percent of the nation's black students in 1984–5, awarded 34 percent of the baccalaureate degrees earned by blacks (Wilson and Melendez, *Minorities in Higher Education: Sixth Annual Status Report*, 8). These figures may suggest, among other things, how essential it is to institutional success in this area to have at least a critical mass of minority faculty and minority student enrollments.

342. Wilson and Melendez, *Minorities in Higher Education: Sixth Annual Status Report*, 23.

343. Kauffman, ed., *Minority Teacher Recruitment and Retention*, 17–18.

344. See also Fields, "Poor Test Scores Bar Many Minority Students From Teacher Training," A32.

345. Lee Daniel, "Many Minority Teachers Plan to Quit, Poll Finds," *New York Times*, 5 October 1988, E5.

346. Rene Sanchez, "Instilling Students with a Love for Teaching," *Washington Post*, 17 October 1988, 1.

347. "Students Give Teaching Low Rating," *Higher Education and National Affairs*, 17 October 1988, 6.

348. Franklin Wilbur, et al., *The National Directory of School-College Partnership: Current Models and Practices* (Washington, D.C.: American Association of Higher Education, 1987), 40.

349. *Ibid.*, 75–77.

350. *Ibid.*, 13–28.

351. "Recruiting Outstanding Students for the Teaching Profession," presentation at AACTE annual meeting, New Orleans, Louisiana, 1988.

352. Denise K. Magner, "Blacks and Whites on the Campuses: Behind Ugly Racist Incidents, Student Isolation and Insensitivity," *Chronicle of Higher Education*, 26 April 1989, A28.

353. Wilson and Melendez, *Minorities in Higher Education: Sixth Annual Status Report*, 13.

354. Cheryl Fields, "Close to 100 Pct. of Grambling U. Students Now Pass Teacher Certification Examination, Up From 10 Pct." *Chronicle of Higher Education*, 23 November 1988, A23–24.

355. Wilson and Melendez, *Minorities in Higher Education: Sixth Annual Status Report*, 13.

356. *Degrees and Other Formal Awards Conferred, 1984–5*, Table 183.

357. Grandy, "Trends in SAT Scores and Other Characteristics of Examinees," 20D, 20E, 22D, and 22E.

358. *Ibid.*, 25D and 25E.

Chapter 9. A Survey of Certification Programs

359. The principal AAC consultants were Ann Converse Shelly, professor of education and director of teacher preparation programs at Bethany College, and Michael Useem, professor of sociology and director of the Center for Applied Social Sciences at Boston University.

We used information supplied by the colleges and universities responding to the survey to arrive at the following for each institution:

☐ The total number of arts and sciences majors graduating during academic year 1985–86 who were recommended for teacher certification

☐ The total number of arts and sciences students recommended for certification during academic year 1985–86 figured as a percentage of the total number of baccalaureate arts and sciences degrees granted during academic year 1985–86

☐ The trend, as measured over the period 1982–1986, in the number of arts and sciences majors recommended for teacher certification

☐ A comparison, with respect to academic ability as measured by standardized tests, of arts and sciences majors who pursue teacher certification with arts and sciences majors who do not.

This information was used in the following way to arrive at our three tiers:

☐ Using the total number of arts and sciences students recommended for teacher certification during academic year 1985–86, we divided the list of institutions into even thirds. The third containing those schools with the most students recommended for teacher certification were awarded two points; those in the middle third were awarded one point; and those in the bottom third were awarded zero points.

☐ Using the percentage calculated in the second item above, we divided our list of institutions into fifths. Those with the highest percentages were awarded four points, with three, two, one, and zero points awarded to each successively lower fifth.

☐ Institutions at which the number of arts and sciences students recommended for teacher certification had increased over the four-year period were awarded two points. Schools where the number had remained approximately the same were awarded one point, and schools indicating a declining number of such students were awarded zero points.

☐ Institutions rating arts and sciences students pursuing teacher certification as academically more able, as measured by standardized tests, than their arts and sciences counterparts not pursuing teacher certification were awarded four points. Institutions reporting no difference in the academic ability of these two groups were awarded two points. Institutions indicating either less ability on the part of arts and sciences students pursuing teacher certification or no opinion on the matter were awarded zero points.

This scheme gives more weight to the relative program size and relative student ability measures than to the absolute program size or program enrollment trends measures. It produced three tiers, constituted as follows:

Tier	Total Institutional Points
Upper (20 percent)	8–12 points
Middle (60 percent)	4–7 points
Lower (20 percent)	0–3 points

360. Because these findings were themselves used to construct tiers, they could not be analyzed by tier.

361. Because these findings were themselves used to construct tiers, they could not be analyzed by tier.